Yesterday, Today and Tomorrow

Yesterday, Today and Tomorrow
The Best of Australian Food

Compiled by
Food Media Club Australia Inc.

Photography
Alan Benson — *Yesterday*
Mil Truscott — *Today*
Brett Stevens — *Tomorrow*

Lothian
BOOKS

Thomas C. Lothian Pty Ltd
132 Albert Road, South Melbourne, Victoria, 3205
www.lothian.com.au

National Library of Australia
Cataloguing-in-Publication data:

Food Media Club Australia Inc.
Yesterday, today and tomorrow; The best of Australian food

ISBN 0 7334 0541 3

1. Cookery, Australian. I. Food Media Club Australia.

641.5994

Designed by The Modern Art Production Group
Colour reproduction by Digital Imaging Group, Port Melbourne
Printed in China by Leefung-Asco
Photography by Alan Benson, Mil Truscott, Brett Stevens
Some accessories provided by The Art of Food & Wine, Woollahra; GL Auchinachie
& Son, Woollahra; Bisanna Tiles, Surrey Hills; Peppercorn, Berrima; Jane Sacchi
Linens, UK.

Editor's note:
Recommended oven temperatures and cooking times in this book apply to
conventional ovens unless otherwise indicated. However every oven is different.
Oven temperatures may vary by up to 20°C if using a fan-forced oven, unless
the fan can be turned off during cooking.

Compiled by:

FOOD
MEDIA
CLUB
AUSTRALIA

Dedication

To those inspirational food writers who have gone before, paving the way, to the current practitioners and to those who follow. May we all make food and the community of the table ever more central to our Australian culture.

Foreword

It must have been 3 years ago. It was Easter and I was at the front of my restaurant one lunchtime, feeling particularly optimistic. The sun was streaming through the windows overlooking the quay and the piles of lobster pots that had been scraped of barnacles during the winter, ready to go back into the sea for a new season. We had fresh brown crab, langoustines and some excellent Dover sole and John Dory on the menu. I often think of such cheerful days by the sea as Australian days, and bumping into a young couple from Sydney, so enthusiastic about my seafood, capped it all for me that day.

But they were curious; they had been living in Surrey for a couple of years and were amazed how indifferent the food was in the suburban areas around their house. British cooking, they did not like. They expressed a homesickness for Australian cuisine.

I'm not naturally given to bouts of defence of my country but it slightly stung me. I pointed out that Australian cuisine probably meant something completely different to me than it did to them. For me it meant memories of the established cooking in the '60s — roast pumpkin with roast lamb, breakfasts of grilled mutton chops with thick gravy, lamingtons, mince with rather overcooked vegetables, round meat pies (more gravy than meat) with peas, Tasmanian scallops in batter from the fish-and-chip shop in Kirribilli, Chico rolls and a feast of frozen rock lobster I had one day in Alice Springs. If, I was moved to point out, they were talking about the fantastic ethnic cuisine, which is now so prevalent everywhere in Australia, then they were talking about some of the best cooking in the world, but Australian cuisine, I didn't think it was worth shouting about.

Looking through the pages of this excellent book, I am moved to think that I was not quite right. True the book is filled with recipes from other countries — Sydney Pemberton's memory of beetroot soup from Terence Conran's Stockpot in '60s Chelsea in London, John Newton's Tumbet from Mallorca, Elizabeth Chong's Provincial chicken, Stefano de Pieri's Veal scaloppine al limone, Joan Campbell's Japonaise, or Maeve O'Meara's Chicken larb which is straight from Thailand, to name a few. But there is also evidence of an emergent local cuisine in the book too. I find that very exciting. It's a combination of magnificent, easily available ingredients grown locally but with origins from all the world's cuisines and an increasing confidence in the métier of other countries' cooking.

Looking through *Yesterday, Today and Tomorrow*, I was struck by the large number of ingredients that would be regarded as unusual in Britain, but which are obviously quite easy to get hold of in Australia. I noticed galangal, shrimp paste, beef tendons, gramma pumpkin, bean thread noodles, holy basil leaves, truffled polenta, Lebanese cucumbers, pea eggplants, tom yum paste, enoki mushrooms, pandanus and lotus leaves. These all speak of shops and markets where everything is available.

There's great confidence in using these ingredients in dishes that have a relaxed Australian spareness about them — like Ian Parmenter's Five-spice chicken with lentils, Matthew Evans' I can't believe it's not laksa, Kathy Snowball's Seared squid and prawns with leek and red onion, or Anders Ousback's Slow-cooked chicken that steams chicken in lotus leaves with a stuffing of shiitake mushrooms, coarse sausage and sticky rice.

This is a fascinating book. The work of the leading cooks and food writers of the last 20 years shows how the national cuisine is developing. It's also important. At a time of inevitable globalisation of food, it's vital that countries that have access to good local produce and a pool of intelligent and skilled cooks produce something that is identifiably regional, otherwise, wherever you go, food will become so boringly the same.

Rick Stein
Padstow, UK

Contents

5   Dedication

6   Foreword by Rick Stein

12   Acknowledgements

13   Introduction by Lyndey Milan

Yesterday

18   **Savoury mushroom roulade** Betty Dunleavy

20   **Rustic beetroot soup** Sydney Pemberton

22   **Curried banana triangles** Jan Boon

23   **Dorinda's easy crab cakes** Dorinda Hafner

24   **Twice-cooked oxtail off the bone** Mary Atkins

26   **Tumbet** John Newton

28   **Compote of quail** Alan Saunders

30   **Nonya fish-head curry** Carol Selva Rajah

32   **Paprika rabbit** Jane Tennant

34   **Calabrese-style meatballs and pasta** Jo Anne Calabria

36   **Provincial chicken** Elizabeth Chong

37   **Carpetbag steak** Peter Howard

38   **Greek-style lamb shanks** Tess Mallos

40   **Beef tendons, Canton style** Max Lake

41   **Grandma Hewitson's lamb shank hotchpotch** Iain Hewitson

42   **Veal scaloppine al limone with asparagus** Stefano de Pieri

44   **Ban chang koay (Peanut crumpets)** Siu Ling Hui

46   **Japonaise** Joan Campbell

48   **Gramma pie** Barbara Santich

50   **Chocolate mousse** Sue Bennett

51   **Truffle cassata** Tom Rutherford

52   **Grandmother's bramble cake** Stephanie Alexander

54   **Passionfruit sponge** Maureen Simpson

Today

58 **Kadek's soup** Nigel Hopkins

59 **Prawn and parsley soup** Nick Ruello

60 **Paul Wilson's eggs with truffles and soft polenta** John Lethlean

62 **Oyster omelette** Geoff Slattery

64 **Steamed lemongrass scallops** Lynne Mullins

66 **Yabby and watercress salad** Kirsty Cassidy

68 **Smoked salmon, fennel and blood orange salad** Belinda Jeffery

70 **Seared squid and prawns with leek and red onion** Kathy Snowball

71 **Larb (Thai chicken salad)** Maeve O'Meara

72 **Caramelised onion and anchovy flatbread** David Sly

74 **Ballotine of ocean trout** Peter Doyle

76 **Tuna spaghetti with anchovy breadcrumbs** Anneka Manning

78 **Coriander magic** Jan Oldham

79 **Slow-cooked chicken** Anders Ousback

80 **Salmon with caramelised onion and tomato** Christine Salins

82 **Smoked trout patties with lime sauce** Barbara Northwood

83 **Stir-fried crayfish with chilli and black beans** Margaret Johnson

84 **Five-spice chicken with lentils** Ian Parmenter

86 **Barramundi poached in coconut milk** Neil Perry

88 **Crusted prawns with fennel and Persian feta salad** Belinda Franks

89 **Thai green chicken curry** Neale Whitaker

90 **Rosemary-scented lamb cutlets** Jan Power

92 **Chilli mango chicken with coriander noodles** Brigid Treloar

94 **Mud crab tom yum** Cherry Ripe

96 **Roasted quail with pea mousseline** Suzanne Gibbs

97 **Mustard seed lamb** Elise Pascoe

98 **Pride of Andalucia** Margaret Fulton

100 **Mango and berry trifle** Gabriel Gaté

102 **The ultimate chocolate cake** Joanna Savill

104 **Iced chocolate fruit pudding** Annette Forrest

105 **Roast hazelnut brownies** Janelle Bloom

106 **Spiced pistachio honey bites** Kay Francis

Tomorrow

110   **Black pepper chicken tea** Christine Manfield

112   **Garfish nigiri-zushi** Hideo Dekura

114   **Crispy fish skin and nori** Fiona Hammond

115   **Chorizo and beans on toast** Jeremy Ryland

116   **Duck and lychee salad** Barbara Lowery

118   **Seafood soufflés with Thai flavours** Charmaine Solomon

119   **Duck egg pasta with kangaroo prosciutto sauce** Maggie Beer

120   **Tuna tartare with Melba toast** Loukie Werle

122   **Prawn and beetroot risotto with saffron mayonnaise** Steven Snow

124   **Spaghetti with radicchio sauce** Simon Johnson

126   **Spaghetti with green tomato sauce** Sue Fairlie-Cuninghame

127   **I can't believe it's not laksa** Matthew Evans

128   **Barramundi in banana leaves with curried chickpeas** Luke Mangan

130   **Duck with star anise and date purée** Di Holuigue

132   **Roasted rack of lamb with miso** Tetsuya Wakuda

134   **Quail in pandanus leaves** Jacques Reymond

136   **Pork with Chinese flavours** Lyndey Milan

138   **Bernard's best pumped rack of lamb** Bernard King

139   **Beef with caramelised onions and mustard sauce** Jenny Sheard

140   **Roast chicken crusted with Australian spices** Ian Hemphill

142   **Sugar 'n spice oxtail** Kate McGhie

144   **Crushed raspberry semifreddo** Donna Hay

146   **Hot pavlovas with Frangelico sauce and praline** Pamela Clark

148   **Goat's milk panna cotta with Champagne jelly** Steve Manfredi

150   **Liqueur fruit ice-creams with macerated cherries** Jan Purser

151   **Chocolate chilli truffles** Victor Pisapia

152   **Macadamia coconut syrup cake** Sheridan Rogers

154   **Biographies**

164   **Glossary**

172   **Index**

Acknowledgements

As with all things, this book is a co-operative effort. My thanks first and foremost to all past and present members of the Food Media Club Australia. What a wonderful contribution you have all made!

To the Executive Committee who agreed immediately to my proposal for such a book, and agreed on the Club's behalf to underwrite the costs of styling and photography, thank you for your support. Royalties will be ploughed back into the Club for educational initiatives.

To each of the contributors to the cookbook, thank you so much for your generosity, your cooperation and your wonderful recipes.

To the teams that undertook the cooking, styling and photography for each section — Michelle Thrift, stylist Mary Harris and photographer Alan Benson for 'Yesterday'; Christine Shepherd, stylist Penny Hurley and photographer Mil Truscott for 'Today'; and Tracey Meharg, stylist Sally Parker and photographer Brett Stevens for 'Tomorrow' — our thanks for their professionalism, commitment and creativity. The results speak for themselves.

To all those who have worked tirelessly behind the scenes, thank you. Special thanks to Kay Francis and Barbara Lowery for collating and checking recipes, and to Anneka Manning, Ian Hemphill, Anushiya Selva Rajah and Carol Selva Rajah for their help in compiling the glossary. To Kirsty McKenzie, our wonderful editor, who has painstakingly worked through the manuscript and patiently drawn it all together, her efforts are very much appreciated by us all.

And finally to our publisher, friend and colleague Averill Chase of Lothian Books for her perseverance, good humour and attention to detail.

You have all made it happen!

Introduction

Today, Australia is universally regarded as being at the forefront of world cuisine with food that is fresh, vibrant and cooked in myriad styles, reflecting our diverse multicultural society. Yet this has not always been the case. The development of our status as a world culinary leader has been a colourful and at times leisurely journey, in part influenced by migration. Indeed, the most rapid changes to our international culinary prowess have taken place during the last 20 years or so. This co-incides with the emergence of quality magazines, newspaper columns and supplements, radio segments and television programs dedicated to disseminating information about food, wine and lifestyle.

Before European settlement took place in 1788, there was a strong indigenous Australian cuisine. Ecologically sustainable and centuries old, uniquely developed in isolation, the unfamiliar flavours of Australia's indigenous food proved of little interest to European settlers. They tried to continue their European traditions, culinary and otherwise. However, conditions were primitive, supplies from the 'old world' sporadic, and the harsh environment often proved incapable of supporting the cultivation of European produce. So available ingredients were substituted. Thus our great tradition of borrowing and adapting had begun.

As a new nation, in terms of European settlement, and unconstrained by any documented or chartered food tradition (à la Escoffier), we have been able to develop our own culinary identity through experimentation and improvisation, borrowing ideas from other culinary traditions. Today, many Australian cooking techniques and ingredients reflect the make-up of our pluralist society.

Australian food is now truly multicultural, influenced by successive waves of migration, Australians' fondness for travel, the availability and affordability of fresh produce and the Australian character, which has always been willing to experiment and adapt and 'have a go'.

Not only has Australia witnessed a growing demand for ingredients and flavours valued by migrant groups, it has also provided the perfect environment for migrants to prosper, unfettered by the traditional constraints of their homelands. Tetsuya Wakuda, for example, insists he could not have achieved in Japan what he has been able to achieve here. He is now proudly Australian and credits his very Australianness with being able to create his unique style. Moreover, for those born in Australia, the irreverence of the Australian character cannot be underestimated. If an Escoffier **had** told us how to do it, we probably would have ignored such instructions anyway!

Just as the Australian wine industry has not been shackled by centuries of tradition and regulation, so it was Australia that first saw fusion food — a style French in basis yet Asian influenced that only succeeds when the creator innately understands both cuisines. Little wonder that today 70% of Australian households own a wok! Meat and three veg may still form part of some Australians' diets, but it is now just part of an eclectic whole. And at last, as part of the broadening of the Australian palate, we are beginning to see a recognition of indigenous Australian products.

In 1982, the Food Media Club Australia was formed as an association of food professionals, dedicated to celebrating the variety and quality of Australian food experiences. Its members have been major players in shaping Australian food culture over the past 20 years.

The Food Media Club's common bond is a love of food and a willingness to share information. It seeks to communicate food issues and to create an environment in which food is central to Australian culture. Little wonder that the dramatic expansion of the food media in Australia should be mirrored by the explosion of interest in Australian food internationally. Australian food and wine magazines and cookbooks have become highly sought after internationally for their recipes, photography, style and layout, which are as fresh and immediate as the food they show. As new crops and ingredients become available in Australia — made possible by our huge landmass and varied climates — it is the food media that informs an increasingly interested and food-literate public, filtering information down the food chain from the high-end chefs to the home cook.

To mark the Food Media Club's 20th birthday celebrations, we chose the theme 'Yesterday, Today and Tomorrow'. The impetus for this was our pride in the Club's achievements and a concern that age and experience are increasingly cast aside on the altar of youth. There is much to be said for experience and knowledge born of maturity, both in the wider community and in the food media. Our aim in our birthday celebrations and in our future vision for the Club has been to recognise and harness this talent, as well as acknowledge the new and vibrant ideas that will carry the Club, and Australian cuisine, forward.

So this book was conceived: to build on and respect the past while embracing the future, to leave behind something tangible, to reward excellence and the generosity of spirit that is at the heart of our industry, and to move food more firmly to the centre of Australian culture.

Organised thematically, the book is a lasting legacy of what has been achieved in food in Australia in the past 20 years, the book charts the path from food styles based on ingredients and concepts from overseas, to food that recognises the diverse nature of contemporary Australia and showcases our incredible range of fresh produce. It honours those who have paved the way, as well as acknowledging the high standard of contemporary food writing, and looks forward to what the future may bring.

Leading Australian food writers, principally Club members, who have contributed to the pre-eminence of Australian cuisine over the last 20 years, have joyfully provided recipes for the book. They represent all sectors of the Australian food media — from newspapers and magazines to radio and television and more recently the Internet. Some names are already well known and loved, others will become so. Chefs and cooks, their recipes are here for all to enjoy.

Lyndey Milan
President
Food Media Club Australia Inc

yesterday

'...it is absolutely vital for all genuine Australian culinary traditions, and particularly regional specialities, to be recognised and accorded due value.'
Barbara Santich

Savoury mushroom roulade Betty Dunleavy

Late in the '70s I devised this recipe using the then new but popular form of soufflé called a roulade when I was preparing a cookbook for the Mushroom Growers' Association. It became one of my favourite recipes for demonstration for charity organisations and television programs. The dramatic preparation of the dish, which required the rolling of the delicate baked soufflé mixture with different fillings, always seemed to create interest and applause. It is also a versatile dish, which can be served hot, at room temperature or cold and adapted with different flavourings and garnishes.

Method *Preheat oven to moderate (180ºC).*

1. Grease and line shallow Swiss roll pan with non-stick baking paper; dust with half the crushed biscuits.

2. Melt butter in medium saucepan over moderate heat. Stir in flour until well blended and bubbling lightly. Remove from heat, gradually stir in milk. Reheat slowly, stirring until mixture is smooth and thick. Simmer 1 minute.

3. Stir in egg yolks and cheese. Adjust seasonings, cover and leave aside until just warm.

4. Meanwhile, beat egg whites in small bowl with electric mixer until foaming but not too stiff. Fold in egg and cheese mixture carefully.

5. Spoon soufflé mixture into prepared pan, spreading lightly but evenly over base of pan.

6. Bake in preheated oven 40–45 minutes. Care should be taken with the baking time; too soft and the roll will collapse, too firm and the roll may crack.

7. To make filling: Melt butter in medium saucepan until foaming; add bacon, cook, stirring, 2–3 minutes. Add mushrooms, cook 2 minutes, stirring occasionally. Add soup, sour cream and pepper; stir to combine. Leave aside, covered, to keep warm.

8. To assemble: Working quickly, place a large sheet of non-stick baking paper on flat surface and turn the cooked soufflé carefully onto it. Remove baking paper from top of soufflé; sprinkle surface with remaining crushed biscuits.

9. Spread mushroom filling lightly over biscuits and quickly but carefully, starting at one end and using the paper as a support, roll the soufflé up as a Swiss roll. Cut into thick slices to serve.

Chef's tip

Filling variations include drained, flaked canned tuna or salmon mixed with a thick white sauce seasoned with gherkins, capers and onion; mix chopped cooked chicken with curried white sauce; chopped ham, with asparagus and condensed asparagus soup.

Ingredients *Serves 6*

¾–1 cup (120–160 g) finely crushed savoury biscuits
60 g butter
2 tablespoons plain flour
2 cups (500 ml) milk
5 eggs, separated
1 cup (120 g) grated tasty cheese
salt and cayenne pepper, to taste

Filling

60 g butter
200 g finely chopped lean bacon
1½ cups (200 g) finely chopped mushrooms
1 x 275 g can condensed mushroom soup
1–2 tablespoons sour cream
black pepper, to taste

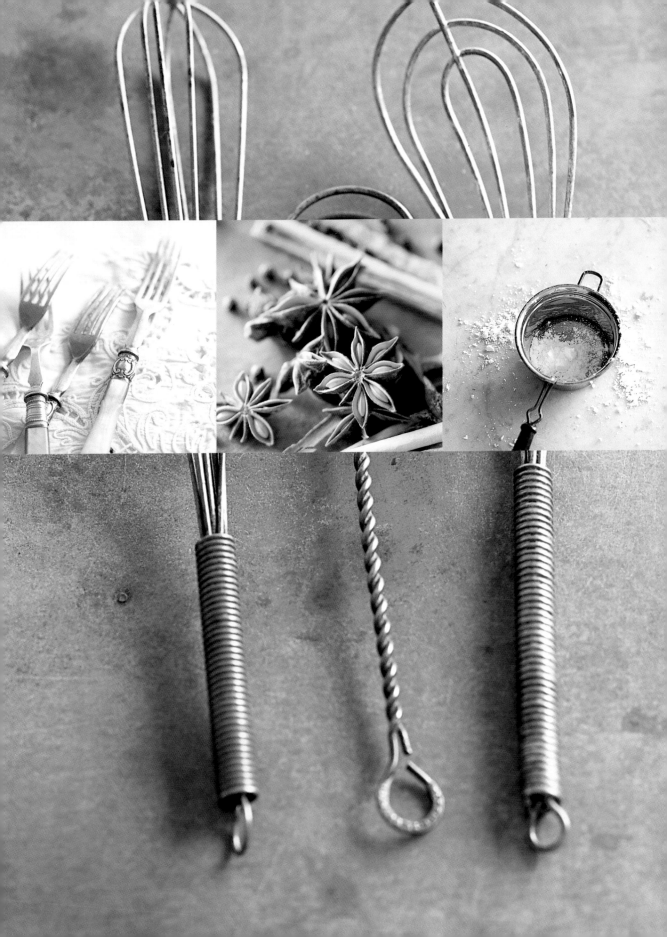

Rustic beetroot soup *Sydney Pemberton*

After leaving home to flat-share in London, a chain of inexpensive eateries called Stockpot provided bottomless bowls of soup to warm the soul. My rustic beetroot soup is a burst of delicious, deep warming pink on a cold day, a comfort food providing memories of my mother's soup prepared with vegetables from the garden. Instead of the traditional swirl of cream I like the sharpness of yoghurt to finish.

Method

1. Heat oil in large saucepan; add bacon, cook, stirring occasionally, 3–4 minutes. Add onion, leek and carrot, cover, cook gently 4–5 minutes, or until vegetables soften.

2. Meanwhile, cut leaves and stalks from beetroot, shred about 1 cup of smaller leaves and stalks finely; leave aside. Peel beetroot, grate coarsely; add to saucepan. Cook, stirring, 2–3 minutes.

3. Add sherry, beef stock, vinegar and tomato, season with salt and pepper. Cover; bring to a boil. Reduce heat, simmer 30 minutes, adjust seasonings.

4. Remove a third of the soup from saucepan and purée in food processor or blender. Return puréed soup to saucepan, bring to a boil; stir in reserved shredded beetroot leaves and stalks, simmer 5 minutes.

5. Serve in bowls topped with baby beetroot leaves.

Ingredients *Serves 6*

1 tablespoon light olive oil

100 g bacon, rind removed, chopped finely

1 large onion (200 g), chopped finely

1 large leek (500 g), white part only, sliced thinly

2 large carrots (360 g), chopped finely

1 small bunch beetroot including leaves (1 kg)

$1/4$ cup (60 ml) dry sherry

4 cups (1 L) beef stock

1 tablespoon sherry vinegar

1 cup canned diced tomatoes

$1/2$ teaspoon sea salt and black pepper, to taste

6 young beetroot leaves, for garnish

Curried banana triangles Jan Boon

I selected this as a versatile, easy to prepare recipe in keeping with our busy lifestyles. It's a recipe that I used some 30 years ago yet it is still appropriate today as it uses conveniently prepared products and fresh produce in an interesting combination of flavours and textures. It's also suitable for vegetarians. Plantains could be used in place of the bananas.

Method *Preheat oven to moderately hot (200°–210°C).*

1. Cut puff pastry into 8 triangles and place on oven tray lined with non-stick baking paper.
2. Bake in preheated oven 15–17 minutes or until pastry is golden brown and risen.
3. Split each triangle into two halves; stand on wire rack to cool.
4. To make filling: Melt butter in large saucepan; add curry paste and cook, stirring occasionally, 2–3 minutes.
5. Add banana, chutney, salt and pepper; cook, stirring occasionally, 3–5 minutes.
6. Stir in coconut cream and white wine; cook, uncovered, 2–3 minutes. Leave filling aside. Reduce oven temperature to slow (150°C).
7. To assemble: Divide banana mixture evenly among 8 triangle halves. Top with remaining 8 halves. Place on oven tray; bake, uncovered, 7–10 minutes.
8. Place triangles on individual serving plates. Serve with small carton of natural yoghurt mixed with a grated and salted cucumber and a pinch of cumin or extra mango and ginger chutney.

Chef's tip
The recipe could be prepared as individual flans using either puff or shortcrust pastry. It could also be made into a puff similar to a pastie, baked in a moderate oven (190°C) 15–20 minutes.

Ingredients *Serves 8*

1 sheet frozen butter puff pastry
60 g butter
2–3 teaspoons hot curry paste
6 firm medium bananas (1.2 kg), diced
2 tablespoons mango and ginger chutney
salt and black pepper, to taste
2 tablespoons coconut cream
1 tablespoon dry white wine

Dorinda's easy crab cakes Dorinda Hafner

These have to be the easiest, simplest, indulgent, exotica on a plate! Please only use proper, fresh crabmeat or the fresh-frozen variety; definitely not tinned crabmeat. The difference in taste is HUGE. These crab cakes are light, tasty, ridiculously easy to make and impressive to present. In the summer, life doesn't get much better than crab cakes with a well-chilled glass of sparkling Riesling. With my compliments…Cheers!

Method *Preheat oven to slow (150°C).*

1. Place eggs in medium bowl, whisk lightly. Separate and shred the crabmeat into small pieces using two forks. Add crab to egg; stir in green onion, mayonnaise, chilli sauce and breadcrumbs. Season with salt and black pepper. Cover mixture; refrigerate 45–60 minutes.
2. Using wet hands, mould crab mixture into 12–14 evenly-sized flat, round cakes.
3. Heat oil in medium non-stick frying pan over medium heat. Cook cakes in batches, turning until cooked through and golden on both sides, about 2–3 minutes each side. Drain on paper towel; cover to keep warm until all cakes are cooked. Serve with fresh green salad, fresh tomato salsa and sliced, ripe avocado sprinkled with fresh lime juice, black pepper and a pinch of salt.

Ingredients *Makes 12–14 cakes*

2 eggs
1 cup (250 g) fresh crabmeat
1 tablespoon finely chopped
 green onion
1 tablespoon low-fat
 mayonnaise
3 teaspoons sweet chilli sauce
1¼ cups (90 g) fresh white
 breadcrumbs
salt and black pepper, to taste
olive oil for shallow frying

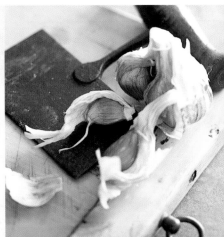

Twice-cooked oxtail off the bone Mary Atkins

In the days of waste not, want not, people learned to appreciate the great value and flavour of the so-called lesser cuts of meat. Oxtail is one of these cuts and it's great for entertaining as it can be prepared well ahead of time. Once made, it will sit happily for 48 hours in the fridge, where the flavours improve. Or you can freeze it. Skim the fat off well as oxtails are inclined to be fatty. You will need two oxtails to make this recipe. The spices and plum jam provide flavour lifts.

Method *Preheat oven to slow (150ºC).*

1. Heat 2 tablespoons of the oil in large frying pan; add onion and garlic; cook, stirring occasionally, until onion softens. Add carrot and celery; cook gently, stirring occasionally, 10–12 minutes, or until vegetables soften.

2. Place 4-litre casserole dish in preheated oven to warm. Meanwhile, place flour in a large plastic bag; season with pepper and ginger. Add several oxtail pieces to bag at a time to dust lightly, leave aside; repeat with remaining oxtail pieces.

3. Transfer onion, garlic, carrot and celery to casserole dish. Return to oven to keep warm.

4. Reheat frying pan; add 1 tablespoon of the remaining oil. Add sufficient oxtail pieces to pan so they can be moved around easily; brown all sides. Remove from pan and leave aside. Repeat with remaining oxtail pieces, adding the remaining oil if necessary.

5. Arrange oxtail over vegetables in casserole dish. Add stock, wine, bay leaf and star anise. Stock should barely cover oxtail — if there is insufficient stock add water. Place sheet of non-stick baking paper between casserole dish and lid and place in oven. Cook 4–5 hours or until meat is tender and falling off bones.

6. Remove dish from oven, allow to cool slightly. Remove oxtail from dish; strain stock and vegetables through metal sieve into a large jug or bowl, pushing through as much pulp as possible; discard solids. Remove meat from bones and leave aside in medium bowl. Discard bones. Remove visible fat and round gristly tendons and discard.

7. Refrigerate meat and stock at least 24 hours. When stock sets, skim surface fat and discard. Remove and discard any surface fat from meat.

8. Bring stock to a boil in medium saucepan; reduce heat, simmer 10–12 minutes, or until sauce is reduced to a syrupy consistency. Add meat and jam to pan, stir until meat is heated through. Adjust seasonings.

9. Arrange meat in centre of serving plates; spoon sauce around meat. Serve with pasta and whole roasted shallots.

Ingredients *Serves 4–6*

4 tablespoons olive oil
1 large onion (200 g), chopped finely
2 cloves garlic, crushed
1 medium carrot (120 g), chopped finely
1 trimmed stick celery (75 g), chopped finely
1 cup (150 g) plain flour
1 tablespoon ground black pepper
1 teaspoon ground ginger
1.5 kg oxtail pieces
2 cups (500 ml) veal or vegetable stock
2 cups (500 ml) red wine
1 bay leaf
2 star anise
1 tablespoon plum jam

Tumbet John Newton

All around the Mediterranean, there's a version of this dish, using some combination of eggplant, capsicum, garlic and tomato. The French call it ratatouille; the Italians peperonata; the Tunisians mechouia. The Mallorquins add potato and call it tumbet. To my mind, it's the pick of the bunch.

I once served this to a friend who, the very next day, sent me a poem of praise, the first line of which read 'Tumbet was yumbet' — although I should add that it's pronounced 'toombet'. But either way, it is most certainly yumbet. Serve hot or cold, on its own or with mahi mahi, red emperor or tuna steaks, with robust spicy sausages or fried liver.

Method *Preheat oven to moderate (180°–190°C).*

1. To make tomato sauce: fry onion in olive oil until soft and transparent. Add tomato, garlic, red wine and pepper; bring to a boil. Reduce heat, simmer, stirring occasionally, until sauce is half its original volume and thick and dark. Stir in thyme or oregano. Then rinse and pat dry with paper towel.

2. Meanwhile, sprinkle eggplant with salt; leave aside 30 minutes.

3. To make tumbet: heat 2 tablespoons of the olive oil in heavy, wide frying pan (preferably earthenware or cast iron); cook potato in batches, both sides, until browned lightly, drain on paper towel. Repeat process with 2 tablespoons of the remaining oil and eggplant, then remaining oil and capsicum.

4. Spread a small amount of tomato sauce over base of deep ovenproof dish, arrange potato on base; top with eggplant, a little more tomato sauce then capsicum.

5. Pour tomato sauce over vegetables and bake, uncovered, in preheated oven 20 minutes. Serve with crusty bread and olive oil.

Chef's tips

• Use sweet potato or turnip instead of potato — turnip is excellent.

• Substitute torn fresh basil for thyme/oregano.

• Make tomato sauce by frying chopped garlic and onion if the whole garlic cloves worry you, but remember, whole cloves gently stewed like this go soft and sweet and are a delicious vegetable.

Ingredients *Serves 6–8*

Tomato sauce

2 medium onions (300 g),
   sliced thinly

2 tablespoons Spanish
   extra virgin olive oil

6 large tomatoes (1.5 kg), peeled
   and diced

1 head garlic, cloves peeled

1 cup (250 ml) red wine

black pepper, to taste

1 tablespoon fresh thyme or
   1 teaspoon dried oregano

Tumbet

2 medium eggplants (600 g), cut
   into 1 cm-thick slices

salt to extract bitterness from
   eggplant

$1/2$ cup (125 ml) Spanish
   extra virgin olive oil

3 large potatoes (900 g), cut into
   1 cm-thick slices

4 large red capsicum (800 g),
   quartered

Compote of quail Alan Saunders

The first French restaurant in Australia was opened at Parramatta in the early nineteenth century. This is the sort of thing they might have served. It comes from the seventh edition of *The French Cook,* published in 1822 by Louis Eustache Ude, who had worked as chef for Louis XVI, the Earl of Sefton and a gentlemen's club in London. I have adapted the recipe a bit — so the quail go into a modern oven rather than a Georgian stew pan — but I have been careful not to make it healthier. If this troubles you, substitute olive oil for the melted butter. It serves two as a main, though if you really want to go for the full period effect, it should be just one of a number of dishes at a dinner for four or more.

Method *Preheat oven to moderately hot (200°–210°C).*

1. Brush quail with 1 tablespoon of the melted butter, roast in pre-heated oven 25 minutes. Turn off oven; rest, covered, 25 minutes.
2. Meanwhile, sauté bacon in remaining melted butter in small frying pan, leave aside and keep warm.
3. Melt extra butter in large frying pan; add flour (working it in slowly and carefully so that the mixture does not go lumpy). Stir in about half the beef stock.
4. Add vegetables and parsley and cook slowly, adding more stock as necessary.
5. When vegetables are cooked, strain cooking liquid into a heatproof jug; reserve vegetables. Adjust seasonings in sauce.
6. Arrange vegetables and bacon on warmed serving dish and place quail on top. Pour sauce over quail.

Ingredients *Serves 2*

4 quail
2 tablespoons butter, melted
4 bacon rashers, chopped
  coarsely
125 g butter, extra
1 tablespoon flour
1/2 cup (125 ml) beef stock
4 large mushrooms (250 g),
  halved
4 spring onions, trimmed
2 small white onions (160 g)
  chopped coarsely
2 sprigs parsley

Nonya fish-head curry Carol Selva Rajah

Fish-head curry (not for the faint-hearted) is an authentic Nonya recipe. Snapper head is popular in Asia because the large bulky head of the fish has soft, moist and flavoursome meat around the cheeks and in and around the eyes. When cooked, it's soft gelatinous and fleshy.

Only the fingers or chopsticks should be used to enjoy this dish. Metal forks and knives were never meant for anything as exotic as this. If you're uncomfortable about cooking the head with the eyes intact, your fishmonger will remove them. Insert a small pickled onion or garlic in the socket instead.

There is a belief that kidnappers feed their prisoners a whole fish and if they start on the head and leave the rest of the fish, then they must be millionaires. The recipe may be adapted to use fish fillets, whole whiting or larger whole fish. Before preparing the dish, it might be helpful to read the Chef's tips at the end of the recipe.

Method

1. Cut fish head cross section, almost butterflied so it will cook quickly and evenly.

2. Combine lemongrass and galangal in food processor or blender and process to a paste.

3. Heat oil in wok or earthenware pot (about 35 cm wide); add shallot or onion and garlic, cook until golden. Add lemongrass and galangal and cook until caramelised and aromatic, about 2–3 minutes over medium heat.

4. Add sambal oelek and turmeric; cook, crumbling shrimp paste (if using) into the mixture and stirring, 1 minute, or until aromatic.

5. Add warmed stock, tamarind purée and half the Vietnamese mint; simmer, stirring, about 3 minutes or until flavours mature.

6. Reduce sauce on medium heat. As flavours develop, note consistency, which should not be too thick at this stage.

7. Lower in the two pieces of fish head. Ideally, the curry liquid should cover the fish; the liquid may be reduced later. Cook over medium heat, until fish is opaque (it will cook very quickly and may break up if overcooked).

8. Reduce heat to simmer; cook about 2 minutes or until sauce reduces. Adjust seasonings, add pepper, salt or fish sauce and sugar only if flavours require balancing. The sour flavours are best when not tampered with. Sprinkle with remaining Vietnamese mint and fried onions. Serve with hot rice and steamed greens.

Ingredients *Serves 4–6*

- 1 large fish head (approx 800 g–1 kg), preferably snapper, cleaned and scaled
- 3 sticks lemongrass, white part only, chopped coarsely
- 2 cm galangal, peeled and chopped coarsely
- 2 tablespoons peanut oil
- 15 shallots (180 g) or 1 medium red onion (170 g), sliced thinly
- 2 cloves garlic, chopped coarsely
- 2 tablespoons sambal oelek, or to taste
- 1 cm fresh turmeric, grated finely (or crushed in mortar and pestle or 1/2 teaspoon turmeric powder)
- 2 cm shrimp paste, dry roasted over a flame then crumbled (see Chef's tip), optional

3 cups (750 ml) fish stock or
   equal parts water and stock
1½ tablespoons thick tamarind
   purée or 3 cm piece of fresh
   tamarind, made up
   (see Chef's tip)
1 cup Vietnamese mint leaves
pepper and salt or fish sauce
   (and sugar to balance
   if necessary), to taste
fried onions, for garnish

Chef's tips

• To dry roast the shrimp paste: Shape into a ball, skewer on a metal satay stick and grill or roast over flame until aromatic and cooked. Crumble before use.

• To make up tamarind: if using blocks, break off amount. Add ½ cup (125 ml) warm water. Mix with a fork or with the fingers to a thick paste. Strain and discard solids. A non-messy alternative is to use one of the many brands of puréed paste available. Ayam has a great purée concentrate, ready salted and needing only to be spooned into the recipe as instructed.

• The curry pot (not essential): The earthenware belanga or chatty is best for fish curry as flavours are retained. Most traditional Nonya families keep one 'chatty' for meat and another for fish. The pots should be first seasoned for use by immersing completely in water overnight, then left to dry thoroughly. To use, cook over a medium flame with some oil then add onions etc. To wash after use, scrub gently. The pots are reusable after immersion in water for one hour. They are available at Indian or Indonesian shops.

Paprika rabbit Jane Tennant

One icy day we had planned a farewell for an American friend. It was to be a real Australian meal so I chose a family favourite: casseroled rabbit — about to serve, her mate whispered: 'Don't tell her what it is — remember America's Easter Rabbit, Bugs Bunny fetish?' Disaster was averted when I remembered that terrible old joke and said it was underground pheasant! Creamy, mashed potatoes are a natural for disposal of the rich gravies that are part of any rabbit dish.

Method

1. Cut rabbit into serving-sized pieces and place in large dish with one of the onions and wine to cover, stand at least 1–2 hours.

2. Drain rabbit and onion; discard wine. Pat rabbit dry; toss in seasoned flour, shake off excess.

3. Melt butter in a large heavy pan; add onion from marinade and extra onion, cook slowly until onion softens. Stir in paprika, cook gently, stirring occasionally, 10 minutes. Add rabbit, garlic, tomato and sherry, stir to combine.

4. Cover pan and simmer ingredients about 1 hour, or until the rabbit is tender. Just before serving, stir in sour cream (do not allow to boil); top with parsley and lemon zest.

Ingredients *Serves 6*

2 x 1.5 kg rabbits

1 medium onion (150 g), sliced thinly

1 cup (250 ml) white wine

flour for coating

salt and pepper, to taste

2 tablespoons butter

2 medium onions (300 g), sliced thinly, extra

1 tablespoon paprika

1 clove garlic, crushed

1 cup (260 g) canned diced tomatoes

1/2 cup (125 ml) dry sherry

1 cup (240 g) sour cream

2 tablespoons finely chopped fresh parsley

1 tablespoon finely grated lemon zest

Calabrese-style meatballs and pasta Jo Anne Calabria

These little meatballs are especially delicious, a good example of Calabrian frugality and cleverness. It's certainly a recipe of yesterday, one that has been and still is passed from generation to generation. It's southern Italian cooking at its best, made with love and pride. From a few simple ingredients comes a dish that is both soul-satisfying and sublime.

Method

1. To make meatballs: Remove and discard crusts from bread. Tear bread into small pieces and place in small bowl; add milk and olive oil. Leave aside, about 15 minutes, or until bread absorbs most of the liquid. Mix with a fork until smooth.

2. Place garlic and salt on board, using flat blade of knife press down firmly; work garlic to a paste.

3. Combine pork mince, zest, juice, Parmesan cheese, parsley and pepper in a large bowl, add bread mixture and garlic paste. Using hands, bring the mixture together and knead until well combined. Shape tablespoonfuls of mixture into balls. Place on tray and refrigerate, covered, 20 minutes before cooking.

4. To make sauce: Heat oil in large heavy-based frying pan, add onion; cook over medium-low heat, 1 minute or until onion softens but is not coloured. Add tomato pasta sauce, the water, salt and pepper, parsley and chilli, if using. Cook, uncovered, stirring occasionally, over medium-low heat, about 20 minutes.

5. Have tomato sauce at simmering point, not any higher or meatballs may break. Spoon meatballs into sauce; cook uncovered, about 12 minutes or until meatballs are just cooked through. Depending on the pan, meatballs may need to be turned gently while cooking.

6. Meanwhile, cook pasta in large saucepan of boiling water, uncovered, until just tender; drain. Divide pasta among serving bowls and serve with a spoonful of tomato sauce and a few meatballs.

Ingredients *Serves 6*

Meatballs

3 slices thick white Italian-style
    bread
1/2 cup (125 ml) milk
2 tablespoons extra virgin
    olive oil
2 cloves garlic, peeled
2 teaspoons salt
500 g pork mince
finely grated zest and juice
    of 1 lemon
1 cup (80 g) finely grated
    Parmesan cheese
1/4 cup coarsely chopped
    flatleaf parsley
ground black pepper, to taste

Tomato sauce

1/4 cup (60 ml) extra virgin
    olive oil
1 small onion (80 g), chopped
    finely
750 ml passata di pomodoro
    (bottled tomato pasta sauce)
1 1/2 cups (375 ml) water
sea salt and black pepper,
    to taste
1 tablespoon finely chopped
    flatleaf parsley
2 small red chillies, optional
500 g pasta (spaghetti, linguine,
    rigatoni or penne)

Provincial chicken Elizabeth Chong

This recipe is my favourite homestyle chicken dish. It is one of the first dishes I cook when I have been away from home a while, perhaps because it brings back memories of childhood days. Whatever the reason, my own children have inherited the same devotion to this old family favourite! It is also a good dish for those watching their diet and for busy people who do not have much time to spend on food preparation. It takes about five minutes to put together, is low in fat, and there is practically no washing up!

Method

1. Wash chicken and chop into large bite-sized pieces. If you include the bones, it will be a tastier dish.

2. Place mushrooms in small heatproof bowl, cover with boiling water, stand 30 minutes. Drain, cut into thin strips.

3. Combine all ingredients in small pie dish or shallow soup bowl; mix thoroughly.

4. Place dish on steaming rack over boiling water in wok, cover wok; steam 25 minutes, or until cooked through. Remove and serve straight from the dish, with steamed rice and green vegetables.

Ingredients *Serves 4*

500 g chicken pieces,
   or chicken wings only

6 Chinese dried mushrooms

1 tablespoon choong toy
   (Chinese preserved turnip)

1 teaspoon finely shredded fresh
   ginger

1 tablespoon light soy sauce

2 teaspoons fish soy (available in
   Chinese stores)

$1/4$ teaspoon salt

2 teaspoons cornflour mixed with
   3 tablespoons water

Carpetbag steak Peter Howard

As far as I know this is an Australian invention — well, we will claim it as ours. It falls into the retro-cooking area and I love it. You can create a variation by using smoked oysters, if you like. Use the tail end of the eye fillet — as it is tapered, the thinner section will be more cooked than the thicker end, delivering greater options to the guests.

Method *Preheat oven to moderate (190°C).*

1. Cut beef fillet lengthways to butterfly it; lay out flat on bench.
2. Heat butter to foaming point in medium frying pan; add mushrooms. Cook 1 minute; add oysters, cook 1 minute.
3. Add lemon juice, zest, peppercorns, brandy and garam masala. Cook 1 minute; remove from heat, sprinkle in enough breadcrumbs to take up juices and make a paste-like filling. Leave aside to cool.
4. Spoon oyster filling down centre of fillet. Wrap meat around filling; tie in place, or skewer fillet closed with toothpicks.
5. Heat extra butter and oil in large frying pan, sear beef all sides. Transfer to rack in baking dish; roast in preheated oven 40 minutes.
6. Remove beef from oven, rest 10 minutes; slice into rounds. Serve with roasted potatoes and freshly steamed greens.

Ingredients *Serves 4–6*

1.5 kg beef fillet
1 tablespoon butter
4 small mushrooms, stems removed, wiped, sliced finely
12 large natural oysters
1 tablespoon lemon juice
1/2 teaspoon finely grated lemon zest
1 teaspoon green peppercorns
1 tablespoon brandy
1/4 teaspoon garam masala
1/2–1 cup (35–70 g) fresh breadcrumbs
1 tablespoon butter, extra,
1 tablespoon olive oil

Greek-style lamb shanks Tess Mallos

Called kapama in Greek, this traditional recipe, redolent with spices, may be made with beef or lamb cubes, or chunky pieces of lamb on the bone. Nowadays I prefer to use lamb shanks — frenched, that is shanks trimmed of excess fat and bone, or untrimmed shanks sawn in two. Long, slow cooking is essential to make the meat moist and succulent. I do not preheat the oven for casseroles — the initial burst of heat in a pre-heated oven is unnecessary for casserole cooking, and it is a small saving on energy.

Method

1. Heat 1 tablespoon of the oil in large frying pan, brown shanks all sides; transfer to casserole dish. Add clove-studded onion, bay leaves and cinnamon stick to dish.

2. Reduce heat under frying pan, add remaining oil and extra onion. Cook gently, stirring occasionally, until translucent, add garlic, cook, stirring, a few seconds; add remaining ingredients. Bring to a boil; pour over lamb shanks.

3. Press a piece of non-stick baking paper on top of shanks, cover dish; cook in slow oven (150°–160°C), about 2–2^1/$_2$ hours, or until meat is almost falling off the bone.

4. Remove baking paper and skim fat from surface. Remove clove-studded onion, bay leaves and cinnamon stick and discard. Serve shanks with pasta or potato mash.

Ingredients *Serves 4*

2 tablespoons olive oil

4 lamb shanks

1 small onion studded with
   3 cloves

2 bay leaves

1 cinnamon stick

1 large onion (200 g), extra,
   chopped coarsely

2 cloves garlic, crushed

425 g can crushed tomatoes

^{1}/$_4$ cup (70 g) tomato paste

1 cup (250 ml) white wine

^{1}/$_2$ cup (125 ml) water

1 teaspoon sugar

salt and black pepper, to taste

Beef tendons, Canton style Max Lake

This is a favourite of mine, from *beef*, (1999). Some find the jellied tendon bits in shin beef or veal delicious, others mistake them for fat, but they are pure protein and highly digestible. 'Lubbly!' Inexpensive, they are obtainable from any Chinese butcher shop. It is the tendon around the kneecap, and sometimes it comes with a small chunk of muscle attached. Beef is preferable to pork, both for size and flavour. They are better if prepared a day ahead, and reheated to serve.

Method

1. Dry roast star anise in small frying pan until fragrant; remove from pan and leave aside.

2. Heat oil in small frying pan. Add onion; cook, stirring occasionally, until golden.

3. Place beef tendons in deep saucepan or casserole, add star anise and onion and enough cold water to cover. Stir in soy sauce and powdered stock; bring to a boil. Reduce heat, simmer uncovered 2 hours, or until tendons are soft. Stir frequently, and check liquid level, adding more hot water if necessary. The tendons will swell during cooking and take up a lot of water.

4. Remove tendons from cooking liquid, leave aside, covered to keep warm. Strain liquid into large heatproof jug; discard star anise. Return liquid to pan and bring to a boil.

5. Rinse noodles under hot water to separate; drain. Cook noodles in the boiling cooking liquid until just tender, drain; divide among serving plates. Serve tendons on noodles with crunchy steamed greens, topped with a splash of oyster sauce.

Ingredients *Serves 4*

10 star anise

1 tablespoon peanut oil

1 medium onion (150 g), chopped coarsely

1 kg beef tendons

2 tablespoons light soy sauce

1 tablespoon powdered chicken stock

375 g packet fresh egg noodles

Grandma Hewitson's lamb shank hotchpotch Iain Hewitson

It is noticeable that the most requested recipes on my *Cooking Adventures* fall into the comfort food category. I don't know whether novelty value has made these seemingly forgotten recipes of yesterday so popular. But whatever the reason, wouldn't it be wonderful to once again come home to a house that is perfumed with the smell of a good old-fashioned stew, braise or even soup simmering gently on the stove out back? (And think of the joy if there just happened to be a loaf of homemade bread in the oven to boot.)

Method

1. Heat oil in large heavy-based saucepan or casserole; cook shanks, in batches, until browned all over. Remove shanks from dish and set aside.

2. Add onion, celery, swede and carrot to pan and cook gently 10 minutes stirring occasionally or until vegetables soften.

3. Return shanks to pan, add stock and seasonings. Bring to a boil; reduce heat, simmer gently, about 1½–2 hours or until meat is very tender. Remove shanks and leave aside.

4. Add cauliflower, peas and zucchini; cook, stirring occasionally, 15 minutes. Remove meat from shanks (discarding fat and sinew); cut into dice, return to pan.

5. Add cabbage and parsley, adjust seasonings and bring to a boil. Reduce heat, simmer 5 minutes. Serve hotchpotch in large soup bowls.

Ingredients Serves 6–8

¼ cup (60 ml) vegetable oil

1.5 kg lamb shanks, French trimmed

2 medium onions (300 g), chopped finely

3 trimmed sticks celery (225 g), chopped finely

1 large swede (450 g), chopped finely

3 medium carrots (360 g), chopped finely

4 cups (1 L) chicken stock

salt and black pepper, to taste

½ small cauliflower (500 g), cut into florets

1 cup fresh peas (160 g)

2 medium zucchini (240 g), sliced thinly

¼ medium savoy cabbage (400 g), sliced thinly

2 tablespoons finely chopped parsley

Veal scaloppine al limone with asparagus Stefano de Pieri

This is an old-fashioned dish, but one that always pleases, especially during the summer months. Too often eaten only at daggy Italian restaurants, scaloppine really should belong to the home cook, although there can be areas of Australia where people cannot access tender young veal. A butcher who cannot supply it should be prodded gently to comply or dropped altogether in favour of a more accommodating one. The so-called strap is the best meat for this dish — do not be talked into yearling beef. When cooking for four, it's best to carry out the operation in two stages, keeping the first batch in a very slow (120°C) oven for a few moments.

Method

1. Toss veal in flour to coat lightly; shake off excess. Heat half the butter with half the olive oil in large, non-stick frying pan.

2. When mixture foams, add half the sage and two slices of the veal, side by side. Season lightly. Cook both sides a few seconds. Add half the white wine, let evaporate, add half the lemon juice and half the cream. Cook, stirring, few seconds, transfer veal and sauce to oven-proof dish; cover, keep warm in oven.

3. Clean frying pan; repeat process. When completed, place veal and sauce on a warm platter.

4. Meanwhile, place asparagus in lightly salted boiling water 30 seconds. Drain; place on the platter beside veal, dress with salt and extra virgin olive oil.

Ingredients *Serves 4*

4 veal slices or schnitzels, pounded thinly

plain flour for coating

2 tablespoons butter

2 tablespoons olive oil

8 sage leaves (optional)

salt and pepper, to taste

1/2 cup (125 ml) dry white wine

juice of 1 lemon (approx 1/4 cup)

1/2 cup (125 ml) cream

16 asparagus spears (approx 500 g)

1 tablespoon extra virgin olive oil

Ban chang koay (Peanut crumpets) Siu Ling Hui

This is a much-loved street food snack, made by hawkers in special heavy bronze-lined pans over coals. It is eaten from morning through to the wee hours. However, it isn't sold anywhere in Australia and as it's a dish I love, I reconstructed the recipe with assistance from my mother. Lye water is the secret ingredient that gives the slightly chewy honeycomb-like texture that characterises this dish. You can omit it but you will end up with a fluffy texture. Lye water keeps almost indefinitely. Serve crumpets as a dessert to follow a Malaysian or Indonesian meal, or as a morning or afternoon tea treat.

Method

1. Blend yeast, the lukewarm water, flour and sugar in a small bowl. Leave aside for about 15 minutes or until frothy.

2. Combine extra flour, extra sugar and salt in large mixing bowl. Make a well in centre; pour in egg, melted butter and yeast mixture. Work the flour in, adding the extra water gradually to make a smooth batter. Add lye water and beat vigorously. Leave aside, covered, at least 3–4 hours, at room temperature. Just before cooking, beat the batter vigorously.

3. To make filling: combine peanuts and sesame seeds in medium bowl, mix well. Heat small, heavy cast iron pan over high heat; brush with oil or butter. Pour a ladle of batter into pan; use ladle to spread an almost translucent layer against the side of the pan. The batter at the base of the pan should not be more than 5–8 mm thick. The batter against the side of the pan will set immediately.

4. Once the batter starts to set (it will look like a crumpet), reduce heat; sprinkle a thin layer of sugar over evenly, then a generous layer of peanut-sesame seed mixture. Cook a few more minutes to ensure the batter is completely cooked.

5. Ease the crisp edges away from side of pan with a thin metal spatula; fold crumpet in half. Serve immediately.

Chef's tips

• It is very important to use a heavy pan to cook the crumpets since you need to have it very hot during cooking.

• Batter can be made the day before if preferred — it improves with resting.

Ingredients *Makes 8–10*

1 teaspoon dried yeast
approx $1/4$ cup (60 ml) lukewarm
  water
1 teaspoon flour
1 teaspoon sugar
2 cups (300 g) self-raising flour,
  extra, sifted
2 tablespoons sugar, extra
pinch salt
1 egg, beaten
20 g butter, melted and cooled
approx $1^{2}/3$ cups (410 ml) water,
  extra
2 teaspoons lye water
peanut oil or melted butter to
  grease frying pan

Filling

$1^{2}/3$ cups (250 g) roasted
  peanuts, ground coarsely
$2/3$ cup (100 g) sesame seeds,
  toasted lightly
approx 100 g sugar

Japonaise Joan Campbell

I've always found this recipe to be delicious. It came from one of our earliest *Vogue Entertaining* magazines. It's a simple, straightforward recipe and does not take long to make. Added appeal for busy cooks comes from the fact that it is best made a day in advance and refrigerated until just before serving time.

Method *Preheat oven to moderate (180°C).*

1. Grease and flour 3 oven trays; mark a 20-cm-diameter circle on each tray.

2. Mix almonds, caster sugar and cornflour together in small bowl and leave aside.

3. Beat egg whites in small bowl with electric mixer until soft peaks form; gradually add extra caster sugar, beating until the mixture resembles uncooked meringue. Fold in combined almond mixture.

4. Spoon mixture into piping bag fitted with 1.5 cm icing nozzle. Starting in the centre, pipe a spiral to cover each circle.

5. Place 2 trays on centre shelf of preheated oven and the third on the shelf below. Bake 25 minutes, or until the cake layers are a pale biscuit colour. You may have to move the trays on the lower shelf up to the centre shelf for 5 minutes more cooking time. Stand the trays on wire rack for 10 minutes to cool slightly then loosen layers with large spatula. Allow to cool completely on trays.

6. To make the coffee butter cream: Bring sugar and the water to a boil in a small saucepan; reduce heat, simmer until syrup thickens. Remove from heat; add coffee essence.

7. Place egg yolks in medium bowl; add syrup gradually, beating constantly with electric mixer. Continue beating, add butter, about 1 tablespoon at a time, until well amalgamated. Add more coffee essence to taste if necessary. Refrigerate, covered, until cream is spreading consistency.

8. To assemble cake: Place one cake layer on serving platter; spread with butter cream. Place second layer on top and spread with butter cream. Repeat with third layer; cover side with remaining cream. Sprinkle all over with toasted almond flakes. Refrigerate cake, preferably overnight. Remove 10–15 minutes before serving, dust top lightly with icing sugar.

Ingredients *Serves 8–10*

1¼ cups (155 g) ground almonds
¼ cup (55 g) caster sugar
¼ cup (35 g) cornflour
5 egg whites
⅔ cup (150 g) caster sugar, extra

Coffee butter cream

1 cup (220 g) caster sugar
¾ cup (180 ml) water
1 tablespoon coffee essence
6 egg yolks, beaten lightly
225 g cold butter

To decorate

1 cup (80 g) almond flakes, toasted lightly
icing sugar, for dusting

Gramma pie Barbara Santich

Once or twice every autumn, when I was growing up, my mother would make gramma pie. Sometimes it was a tart, but I think more often a pie, with a thick layer of dense pulp, sweetened and flavoured with lemon and cinnamon, overlaid by a shortcrust pastry lid, crimped around the edges and sprinkled with sugar before baking. Typically, she would make it in one of the rectangular enamelled pie dishes with sloping sides.

Gramma pie might be one of our forgotten regional specialities. In late autumn in the Hunter region of NSW, the crudely lettered signs of roadside stalls announce grammas for sale, and yet they are almost unknown in Adelaide. Our Australian gramma pie — the way my mother made it, and as this 1937 recipe instructs — is quite different to the American pumpkin pie, enriched with eggs and cream. It is distinctively ours, and I offer this recipe because I believe that all genuine Australian culinary traditions, particularly regional specialities, deserve to be recognised and celebrated.

Method *Preheat oven to hot (220°–230°C).*

1. Combine sugar, pumpkin, sultanas, cinnamon, ginger and lemon juice in large bowl. Beat with electric mixer until well combined.
2. Line 22-cm rectangular pie dish with pastry, fill with gramma mixture and cover with pastry. Press pastry edges together, trim and brush with milk combined with extra teaspoon sugar.
3. Bake in preheated oven 20 minutes or until pastry is browned lightly. Remove from oven, sprinkle with extra sugar if desired; serve warm.

Shortcrust pastry

1. Sift dry ingredients together and rub in shortening with finger-tips. Add water a little at a time, to make a dry dough. This should be so dry that the rolled-out dough breaks on attempting to bend it.
2. Roll on a marble slab and cut as required. The odd scraps may be packed together and rolled out again without altering the texture.

Chef's tips
• Pastry should be made in a cool room with cool hands and rolled on a cold slab.
• Butter can be substituted for the lard and clarified fat.

Adapted from recipe from *The Woman's Mirror Cookery Book (A Selection of 2000 Recipes from The Australian Woman's Mirror — With Tables of Food Values by a well-known Lady Doctor) The Bulletin,* Sydney, 1937.

Ingredients *Serves 8*

1 cup (220 g) sugar
$1^{1}/_{2}$ cups (600 g) hot, boiled, mashed gramma pumpkin (or pie-pumpkin)
$^{3}/_{4}$ cup (120 g) sultanas
1 teaspoon cinnamon
$^{1}/_{2}$ teaspoon ground ginger
juice of 1 lemon (approx $^{1}/_{4}$ cup)
1 quantity shortcrust pastry or 2 sheets ready-rolled short-crust pastry
2 tablespoons hot milk
1 teaspoon sugar, extra
extra sugar for sprinkling

Shortcrust pastry
3 cups (500 g) plain flour
1 teaspoon baking-powder
$^{1}/_{4}$ teaspoon salt
1 scant cup (250 g) shortening — equal parts butter, lard and clarified fat
ice-cold water to mix

Chocolate mousse Sue Bennett

Although recipe development is not part of my working life, I am an enthusiastic cook who has, for many years, adapted and created dishes. This is the easiest dessert to prepare and can be made in advance. I always serve it as a dessert option but rarely does anyone say no. You can use flavoured chocolate rather than plain for an interesting variation.

Method

1. Melt chocolate in bowl over simmering water. When almost melted, add butter; stir until smooth. When smooth and melted, remove from heat; stir in egg yolks.
2. Beat egg whites in small bowl with electric mixer until stiff. Fold egg white into chocolate mixture.
3. Divide mousse mixture among six ¹/₂-cup (125 ml) bowls or ramekins. Refrigerate until set.

Ingredients *Serves 6*

200 g Nestlé Club dark
  chocolate
90 g butter, cut into small cubes
6 eggs, separated

Truffle cassata Tom Rutherford

The Truffle cassata was born for the Food Media Club to celebrate their 20th year, using commercial ice-cream, a range of Truffle enhancements, a splash of innovation for an ice-cream cake of celebrated proportions. Sprinkle it with rose petals and a dusting of icing sugar and an historic moment is created.

Method

1. Construct three plastic rings from 5-cm wide food grade plastic strip secured with broad sticky tape. The chocolate layer should be approximately 20 cm in diameter, the strawberry layer about 12-cm diameter and the pistachio layer about 5 cm.

2. Line plate or tray with non-stick baking paper, place 20-cm ring on plate and insert sponge into base. Place other rings on plates lined with non-stick baking paper.

3. Combine strawberries, the water, sugar and lemon zest in bowl of food processor or blender, process until smooth. Transfer mixture to small saucepan; bring to a boil. Reduce heat, simmer, uncovered, until sauce thickens slightly; remove from heat, strain through a fine sieve, leave sauce aside until cool.

4. Combine strawberry ice-cream, extra strawberries, marshmallows and macadamias in medium bowl, swirl strawberry sauce through.

5. Combine ingredients for remaining layers in separate bowls; spoon mixtures into appropriate rings; freeze at least 3–4 hours.

6. To assemble cake: place two smaller rings on top of the chocolate layer in tiers, remove plastic rings. Sprinkle with rose petals; dust with sifted icing sugar.

Chef's tips

• For an even better result, freeze layers overnight before assembling.

• Ready-made pistachio paste is available from The Essential Ingredient, Ph: 02 9557 2388

• Food grade plastic strip for the moulds is available from G & J Food Services, Ph: 02 9555 7750

Ingredients *Serves 20–25*

20-cm round thin sponge cake

Strawberry layer

1 punnet strawberries

1/4 cup (60 ml) water

1/3 cup (75 g) sugar

1 teaspoon finely grated
  lemon zest

1 L strawberry ice-cream

1 punnet strawberries, extra,
  quartered

100 g pink marshmallows, cut
  into 1 cm dice

50 g finely chopped toasted
  macadamias

Chocolate layer

2 L chocolate ice-cream

250 g dark chocolate chips

100 g white marshmallows, cut
  into 1 cm dice

Pistachio layer

500 ml pistachio ice cream

50–80 g pistachio paste

3/4 cup (100 g) finely chopped,
  skinned, toasted pistachios

rose petals and icing sugar,
  to decorate

Grandmother's bramble cake Stephanie Alexander

Whenever I make this cake or pie it elicits groans of delight. It is not just its magnificent flavour but also because the experience of a big, generous golden pie is becoming more and more of a rarity. If you live where there are still some unsprayed blackberries I urge you to make this for your special food lovers. The lard pastry is a speciality of Yorkshire where my grandmother, and this recipe, came from.

Method *Preheat oven to moderately hot (200°–210°C).*

1. To make pastry: Sift flours with salt into medium bowl. Rub lard in quickly. Make well in centre of flour mixture and work in the cold water. Knead quickly 2–3 minutes or until dough is soft, springy and elastic. Form dough into flat disc, wrap in plastic wrap; refrigerate 30 minutes.
2. Roll two-thirds of pastry into circle approximately 26 cm in diameter. Transfer circle on to slightly larger greased ovenproof plate. The pie must be assembled on serving plate as it is impossible to move. Roll remaining third of pastry into a circle about 14 cm in diameter. In both cases the pastry should be rolled about 6 mm thick.
6. Place berries in a heap on larger circle. Pleat sides of pastry around fruit so it resembles a mob-cap. Pleated edges should lean slightly inwards towards berries.
7. Rest smaller pastry circle lightly on top of berries and with edges extending on to pastry pleating. Do not seal the lid or press it down heavily as it has to be removed after baking. As some juice may run during baking, put a metal tray underneath pie plate. Brush pastry with egg wash; bake in preheated oven 25 minutes, or until pastry is cooked and golden brown.
8. Remove pie from oven, lift lid carefully using a flexible spatula (loosen the edges of lid first); add sugar and butter slices. Replace lid and leave pie in warm place at least 10 minutes before cutting into wedges.

Chef's tip
Use a spoon as well as a knife and lifter for serving as there will be plenty of delicious juice that will flow into the pie-plate. Serve with clotted cream or thick farm cream.

First published in *Stephanie's Menus for Food Lovers*, 1985 (currently out of print; a revised edition will be published in late 2003).

Ingredients *Serves 6*

Pastry
1$\frac{1}{3}$ cups (200 g) plain flour, sifted
1$\frac{1}{3}$ cups (200 g) self-raising flour, sifted
pinch salt
200 g lard, at room temperature
$\frac{3}{4}$ cup (185 ml) cold water
1 whole egg mixed with pinch salt (for egg wash)

Filling
2 cups (300 g) blackberries, green stems removed, but not washed
$\frac{1}{2}$ cup (110 g) sugar
60 g unsalted butter, sliced thinly

Passionfruit sponge Maureen Simpson

There has always been a great tradition of cake baking in Australia, and to be a good sponge maker was always considered the ultimate baking skill. This passionfruit sponge is my mother's recipe and one I learned to make as a girl. The secret of success is to beat the eggs and sugar very thoroughly, and to this day I still use her trick of drawing a figure eight with a spoonful of the mixture to test if it's ready.

Method *Preheat oven to moderate (180°–190°C).*

1. Grease two 20-cm-round sponge cake pans well with butter (add a pinch of flour to the butter for a fine crust); line bases with non-stick baking paper.

2. Beat eggs in large bowl with electric mixer until frothy; add sugar, 1 tablespoon at a time, continuing to beat at high speed. When all sugar has been added, continue to beat until mixture is very thick, about 10 minutes. To test if it is beaten sufficiently, take a large spoonful of mixture and draw a figure eight on top of the mixture. The impression should remain for a few seconds.

3. Sift flour and cornflour together; add gradually to egg mixture, one heaped tablespoon at a time, stirring lightly with flat egg whisk until mixed through evenly.

4. Melt butter in the boiling water in cup; stir quickly and lightly through sponge mixture. Divide mixture between prepared cake pans.

5. Bake in preheated oven about 25 minutes or until sponge is springy to the fingertips and shrinks slightly from side of pan. Remove from oven; stand few minutes before turning out on to cake rack to cool.

6. Add icing sugar to whipped cream; stir in vanilla. When cakes are cool, sandwich together with cream. Place on flat serving plate; spread top with passionfruit icing and leave to set.

Passionfruit icing

Mix icing sugar, butter, passionfruit pulp and vanilla together in small bowl. Add few drops boiling water if necessary for good spreading consistency.

Ingredients *Serves 8*

4 eggs
$3/4$ cup (165 g) caster sugar
1 cup (150 g) self-raising flour
1 tablespoon cornflour
2 teaspoons butter
$1/3$ cup (80 ml) boiling water
$2/3$ cup (160 ml) thickened cream, whipped
1 teaspoon icing sugar
$1/2$ teaspoon vanilla essence

Passionfruit icing

1 cup (160 g) icing sugar, sifted
2 teaspoons butter, softened
1 passionfruit
few drops vanilla essence

today

'The best food is simple food done well, relying on sound basics, simple techniques and good ingredients . . . the hallmarks of how we eat today.'
Anneka Manning

Kadek's soup Nigel Hopkins

Occasionally you come across a recipe that is so simple yet so delicious it seems like you've captured some sort of 'life force' in a bowl. That's how I regard Kadek's soup.

My friend Kadek is the owner of the excellent Miro's Garden Restaurant in Ubud, Bali, which he runs with his Australian wife, Joy, and the soup was his creation. In the tradition of 'soto ayam', he adds just a little salt and pepper, but if more oomph is required he might add a mix of fried shallots, garlic, turmeric, ginger and lemongrass. It can be served, if preferred, with a dash of kecap manis (sweet soy sauce).

Method

1. Place noodles in medium heatproof bowl, cover with boiling water, stand until just tender; drain.
2. Combine chicken stock, shredded chicken and salt and pepper in large saucepan, bring the mixture to a boil.
3. Divide noodles, vegetables and herbs among serving bowls, pour over hot stock and chicken mixture. Top with deep-fried shallots.

Ingredients Serves 4

100 g bean thread noodles
6 cups (1.5 litres) chicken stock
1 cup finely shredded
  cooked chicken
salt and black pepper, to taste
2 cups finely shredded cabbage
1 medium carrot (120 g),
  shredded finely or processed
  into fine spirals
1 cup (80 g) bean sprouts
1/4 cup loosely packed coriander
  leaves
1/4 cup loosely packed holy basil
  leaves
deep-fried shallots, for garnish

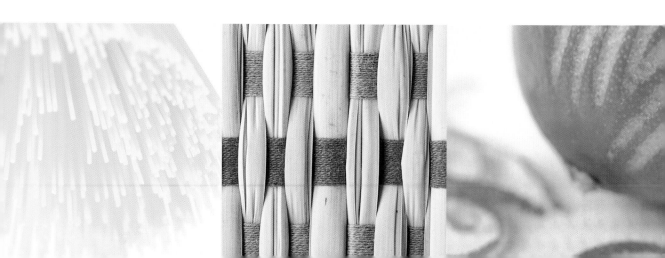

Prawn and parsley soup Nick Ruello

This is a quick and delicious adaptation of a soup my mum made at home; it's easily cooked in a saucepan. Medium-sized prawns are best sliced in half lengthways to bring out their flavour. You can spice this soup up for winter by adding a finely chopped small chilli to the prawns when frying. Serve with crusty bread.

Method

1. Bring chicken stock and water to a boil in medium saucepan or bowl in microwave.

2. Heat butter, oil and garlic in large frying pan; add prawns, cook, stirring, 1 minute, or until prawns just change colour. Stir in cream.

3. Add hot diluted stock, bring to a boil, cook, stirring, 1 minute. Add about three quarters of the parsley, mix well; simmer 5 minutes, stirring occasionally.

4. Divide soup among serving bowls; sprinkle with remaining parsley and pepper.

Ingredients Serves 4

1½ cups (375 ml) chicken stock

1 cup (250 ml) water

2 tablespoons butter or
  margarine

1 tablespoon olive oil

1 clove garlic, crushed

400 g small or medium uncooked
  prawns, shelled

1 tablespoon thickened cream

1 cup flatleaf parsley, chopped
  finely

black pepper, to taste

Paul Wilson's eggs with truffles and soft polenta John Lethlean

I chose this dish for a couple of reasons. For one, it represents an exciting period in the '90s when British chefs were setting new standards in Melbourne. New and ambitious restaurants were springing up and there was a mood of optimism, a willingness to take risks. Paul Wilson, who developed this dish, came here from Quaglino's in London and represented a style remarkably in touch with the Australian culinary vernacular. The creation of this dish also marked a time in my life when I had finally made a decision about what I wanted to do in journalism. I was in the first throes of lust with a job dedicated to food and restaurant reporting at *The Age*, and that, too, was exciting. Paul Wilson is now executive chef of South Yarra's Botanical.

Method

1. Bring stock, garlic and Parmesan trimmings to a boil in medium saucepan. Reduce heat; simmer about 4 minutes or until fragrant with Parmesan. Strain stock through sieve into another pan and heat gently.
2. Add polenta gradually, whisking constantly to a smooth paste. Cook very gently 40 minutes, uncovered, stirring occasionally. Continue stirring; add butter, cream, grated Parmesan and truffle oil. Remove from heat, pass through a sieve; adjust seasonings, cover to keep warm.
3. Poach eggs in large frying pan of simmering water, uncovered, until cooked as desired; drain on paper towel.
4. Divide polenta among serving plates; top polenta with a poached egg. Sprinkle with shaved truffle then shaved Parmesan. Spoon beurre blanc over top and serve immediately with crusty bread.

Beurre blanc

1. Combine shallot, garlic and champagne or vinegar in small saucepan, bring to a boil. Reduce heat, simmer, uncovered, until about 1 teaspoon of the reduced liquid remains.
2. Add wine, reduce by half; add cream, stir to combine and heat through.
3. Whisk in butter, season with salt and pepper, strain mixture through sieve into small jug; discard solids. Stir in truffle oil. Cover and keep warm until serving time.

Ingredients Serves 4

Poached eggs

2 cups (500 ml) vegetable stock
1 clove garlic, crushed
$^1/_4$ cup (20 g) Parmesan cheese
   trimmings (rind etc)
$^1/_3$ cup (55 g) truffled polenta
25 g unsalted butter
1 tablespoon cream
$^1/_4$ cup (20 g) finely grated
   Parmesan cheese
1 tablespoon truffle oil
salt and black pepper, to taste
4 eggs
0.5 g shaved fresh or canned
   truffle (white or black)
1 tablespoon shaved Parmesan
   cheese

Beurre blanc

2 shallots (20 g), chopped finely
1 clove garlic, crushed
1 tablespoon champagne or
   white wine vinegar
1 tablespoon dry white wine
$^1/_4$ cup (60 ml) cream
40 g unsalted butter, cubed
salt and pepper, to taste
1 teaspoon truffle oil

Oyster omelette Geoff Slattery

The creative processes (inspirations or flukes!) which lead to great food can come from the most unlikely sources. This recipe came after a viewing of that wonderful foodies' movie, 'Big Night'. It's an enchanting story of two Italian-American brothers, restaurateurs, fanatical about excellence, unable to cope with compromise. Their business drifts, coughs, splutters, and dies. In the last scene, shot with one camera, in one take, as I recall, the front of house partner makes an omelette. The scene, to my recollection, is shot without words being spoken. The omelette is the final connection, between the brothers and staff. They eat in silence. The credits roll.

I watched this alone, went home to an empty house and found oysters and eggs and spring onions in the fridge. A delicious snack was born. I ate it alone, in silence, thinking of the bonds that food can make.

Method *Preheat oven to moderately hot (200°–210°C).*

1. Break eggs into a medium bowl; whisk furiously until well beaten.
2. Heat olive oil or butter in 15-cm ovenproof frying pan until sizzling. Pour in beaten egg, working to the edges. The egg should seal almost instantly.
3. Add spring onion and oysters, cook, 30 seconds.
4. Place frying pan in preheated oven; bake until set, no more than a few minutes. The centre should be moist, the oysters just warm.
5. Meanwhile, toast bread both sides, spread with butter. Dot top of omelette with butter; sprinkle with parsley and pepper. Serve with buttered toast.

Chef's tips

• The best toast for this dish is brioche, but any decent bread will do, so long as it's not crisp.
• Use a larger pan for making an omelette for more than one. The trick is to achieve an omelette with depth, not one which can fold. The end result is more like the inner part of a quiche than an omelette.

Ingredients *Serves 1*

3 eggs
2 teaspoons olive oil or butter
2 spring onions, chopped
    coarsely
6 shucked oysters
1 thick slice bread
butter for toast and serving
coarsely chopped flatleaf parsley,
    to serve
black pepper, to taste

Steamed lemongrass scallops Lynne Mullins

Scallops are nutritious and delicious, need little preparation and only take a few minutes to cook so are ideal for our busy lifestyles. There are three main species caught in Australia, the edible part is the creamy white muscle and the orange coral, just cut the dark sand track away with a small sharp knife. Serve them in the shell whenever possible as it is the ideal baking dish and container for a sauce. This Asian-style recipe with its delicate sauce accentuates the flavour of fresh plump sea scallops.

Method

1. Loosen scallops from shells with sharp knife.
2. Combine soy sauce, wine, mirin, vinegar, oyster sauce and the water in small bowl; mix well. Add ginger and sugar; stir until sugar dissolves.
3. Working in batches, spoon $1/2$ teaspoon soy mixture on to each scallop; steam, covered, in single layer on rack or in bamboo steamer in wok half-filled with simmering water 1–1$1/2$ minutes or until scallops are just cooked. Repeat with remaining scallops and soy mixture.
4. Drizzle remaining soy mixture over scallops, sprinkle with lemongrass and garlic chives and serve sprinkled with extra garlic chives.

Ingredients Serves 4

20 scallops (with or without roe)
  on the half shell
2 tablespoons light soy sauce
3 teaspoons Chinese rice wine
  (shaoxing)
2 teaspoons mirin
1 teaspoon Chinese black vinegar
1$1/2$ teaspoons oyster sauce
1 tablespoon water
2 teaspoons finely grated
  fresh ginger
1 teaspoon caster sugar
2 tablespoons thinly sliced
  lemongrass
2 tablespoons finely chopped
  garlic chives
garlic chives, extra, to serve

Yabby and watercress salad Kirsty Cassidy

This salad has glamorous spontaneity about it, reflecting my style of food. It is fresh and simple, made with produce that has been thoughtfully sourced, preferably from organic growers. It's a collection of summer ingredients, easy to prepare and served with high visual impact.

Yabbies are the stars of this salad, I think they are so quintessentially Australian and remind me of my holidays spent fishing for bucketfuls of the little critters around the rice canals of the Riverina. Watercress is one of those leafy greens that has a unique flavour and I spot it growing abundantly on my daily coastal walk around the rocky outcrops of Bondi beach. Teamed with a creamy homemade lemon mayonnaise, it's simply Sydney summer on a plate.

Method

1. Place about 5 kgs of ice and 3–4 L of water into a large bowl or sink. Place live yabbies in iced water for approximately 40 mins to 1 hour, or until dead.
2. Combine the water, peppercorns, bay leaves, parsley, onion, salt and lemon juice in a large stockpot; bring to a boil.
3. Remove yabbies from freezer; add to simmering court bouillon over high heat. Cover to return to a boil; remove the lid, simmer 5 minutes or until shells turn orange. Remove from heat, drain; leave yabbies aside to cool.
4. Meanwhile, bring a large saucepan of water to a boil; add asparagus and cook 1 minute or until just tender. Drain asparagus; transfer to large bowl of iced water.
5. Cut cucumbers lengthways into fine strips. Slice avocado, lengthways, into thirds. Drain asparagus. Leave aside until required.
6. To shell yabbies: Twist the head from the tail; discard the head. Use scissors to cut open the undertail shell; remove tail meat.
7. To serve: Arrange three asparagus spears and an avocado piece on each plate. Divide yabbies, watercress and cucumber among plates. Serve each salad with a spoonful of lemon mayonnaise topped with a teaspoon of salmon roe, seasonings to taste and a lemon slice.

Ingredients Serves 6

24 (about 2.3 kg) uncooked yabbies
20 cups (5 litres) water
few peppercorns, bay leaves and parsley sprigs
1 medium onion (150 g)
pinch salt
juice of 1 lemon
2 bunches asparagus (500 g), trimmed
2 Lebanese cucumbers (260 g)
1 medium avocado (250 g), seeded, halved lengthways
4 cups (100 g) watercress sprigs
1 1/2 tablespoons salmon roe
sea salt and black pepper, to taste
lemon slices, for serving

Lemon mayonnaise

2 egg yolks
1/3 cup (80 ml) lemon juice
1 cup (250 ml) vegetable oil
1/2 cup (125 ml) extra virgin olive oil
sea salt, to taste

1. Place egg yolks and lemon juice in bowl of food processor and process until combined.
2. Gradually pour in vegetable and olive oils and continue to process until mayonnaise thickens.
3. Remove from the processor, adjust seasonings; cover and leave aside until required.

Chef's tips

• Freezing or chilling the yabbies puts them to sleep kindly, before the cooking process.
• If you prefer, lay the yabbies out on a tray and place in freezer for 2 hours or longer until dead. You will need a large freezer if you adopt this method as 10 live yabbies can take up a lot of room.
• Leftover mayonnaise can be stored in a sterilised jar in the fridge for up to two weeks.
• Use free-range eggs in the mayonnaise.

Smoked salmon, fennel and blood orange salad Belinda Jeffery

This is a beautiful looking winter salad. The soft pinks and pale greens of the salmon and fennel are offset by the startling intensity of the blood oranges. It's really refreshing and a lovely easy entrée for a special dinner as everything can be prepared well ahead and put together at the last minute. If you can't buy kiln-cooked salmon, you can use regular smoked salmon.

Method

1. Peel oranges, making sure no white pith remains. Cut down between membranes with a sharp knife; remove segments. Remove seeds from blood orange segments.

2. Flake the salmon into chunks (if using regular smoked salmon, slice into narrow strips). Spoon a little orange mayonnaise into the middle of each plate. Place a small pile of fennel on top; then orange segments and salmon. Drizzle a little orange mayonnaise on top; repeat layers.

3. Finish with a little mayonnaise, fennel and blood orange segment. Garnish with mint leaves. Serve remaining mayonnaise separately.

Orange mayonnaise

1. Bring orange juice to a boil in a small saucepan; boil, uncovered, until juice reduces to a couple of tablespoons of syrupy juice. (Swirl pan frequently towards end as it scorches easily.) Leave aside to cool slightly.

2. Blend or process egg; add oil gradually in a thin stream while motor is operating until mixture thickens. Add vinegar, lemon juice, reduced orange juice and salt; process to combine. It will be thinner than regular mayonnaise (it also thickens a little once it's chilled).

3. Taste mayonnaise; adjust salt/lemon/vinegar balance if necessary. Add dash extra orange juice if it doesn't seem quite 'orangey' enough. Transfer to container and refrigerate until serving time.

Ingredients *Serves 6*

3–4 navel oranges, depending on size

3–4 blood oranges, depending on size

3 kiln-cooked (also called hot-smoked) salmon fillets

2 medium fennel bulbs (600 g), halved, cored, sliced finely

mint leaves, for garnish

Orange mayonnaise

1 cup (250 ml) orange juice, strained

1 egg

1 cup (250 ml) light olive oil

$3/4$–1 tablespoon white wine vinegar

3 teaspoons lemon juice

salt, to taste

orange juice, extra (optional)

Seared squid and prawns with leek and red onion Kathy Snowball

I love the fresh, clean flavours of the herbs in this recipe; it is important to add them just before serving so that they don't wilt. Use the freshest produce the growers' markets and providers can supply. This dish is also delicious as a main course, with the addition of cooked cannellini beans.

Method *Preheat oven to moderately hot (200°–210°C).*

1. Combine leek and onion in a large baking dish, toss with 2 tablespoons of the olive oil; roast in preheated oven 30 minutes, or until browned and tender.

2. Cut squid tubes in half lengthways and open out flat with the inner side facing upwards. Score flesh in a criss-cross pattern and cut each piece in two, crossways.

3. Heat remaining olive oil in a large frying pan and cook squid and prawns, in batches, over high heat until just tender. Combine prawns and squid with leek and onion on serving platter, pour two-thirds of the dressing over, toss to combine; leave aside to cool slightly.

4. Just before serving, stir coriander and mint through seafood mixture, drizzle with remaining dressing.

Chilli dressing

Combine lemon juice, olive oil and chilli in screwtop jar or small bowl, adjust seasonings; stand 30 minutes for flavours to develop.

Ingredients *Serves 6*

2 medium leeks (700 g), white part only, cut into 2 cm lengths
2 medium red onions (340 g), each cut into 8 wedges
1/3 cup (80 ml) olive oil
3 medium squid, cleaned
18 medium uncooked prawns (approx 450 g), shelled with tails in tact, deveined
1 cup loosely packed mixed coriander and mint leaves

Chilli dressing

1/4 cup (60 ml) lemon juice
1/2 cup (125 ml) olive oil
2 small red chillies, seeded, chopped finely
salt and pepper, to taste

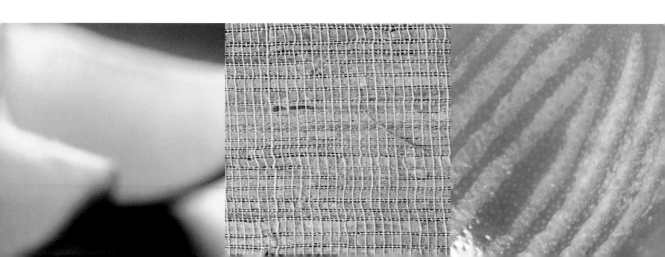

Larb (Thai chicken salad) Maeve O'Meara

I love the simplicity of this dish, which works beautifully as an entrée or with jasmine rice as a main course for summer. The best thing is to have the mint, coriander and Vietnamese basil (the purple stemmed variety) growing, so all you have to do is go to the garden and snip. The toasted rice adds a depth of flavour — this is a technique I saw being used by the Hmong people who emigrated from northern Thailand and settled in Australia. This dish looks pretty with the baby cos carrying the salad like little boats.

Method

1. Place rice in medium frying pan over medium-high heat. Cook, stirring frequently until golden. Leave aside to cool. Place toasted rice in food processor; process until ground.

2. Heat oil in frying pan, add chicken mince and lemongrass and cook, stirring frequently, 7 minutes, or until mince is cooked through. Remove from heat, allow to cool.

3. Add fish sauce, lime juice, palm sugar, shallot, mint, coriander, chilli, peanuts and toasted rice, mix well to combine.

4. To serve: Place cos leaves on serving plate, top with mince mixture and Vietnamese mint.

Chef's tip

Adjust fish sauce, lime juice and palm juice to taste, as required.

Ingredients Serves 4–6

2 tablespoons jasmine rice

2 tablespoons oil

500 g chicken mince

1 stick lemongrass, white part only, chopped finely

2 tablespoons fish sauce

2 tablespoons lime juice

2 tablespoons coarsely grated palm sugar

2 shallots, chopped finely

1/2 cup loosely packed mint leaves, shredded finely

1/3 cup loosely packed coriander, chopped roughly

2 small red chillies, seeds removed and chopped finely

1/3 cup salted roasted peanuts, chopped coarsely

baby cos lettuce leaves, to serve

Vietnamese mint, to serve

Caramelised onion and anchovy flatbread David Sly

Vince Trotta, a Barossa Valley chef at Salter's Restaurant, Angaston, is from a proud line of Italian caterers, and advocates food to share, with soulful, robust flavours. He calls it New Australian food. Nice touch. I love cooking his moreish flatbreads for friends who flop around our living room on lazy Friday evenings, for famished families on cold winter weekends, and as a starter for feasts under the pergola. If you don't like anchovies, use roasted, peeled and sliced capsicum and/or pitted olives.

Method *Preheat oven to very hot (250°C).*

1. Combine yeast and the warm water in small bowl, leave aside until mixture begins to bubble. Combine yeast mixture and baker's flour in large bowl; mix 4–5 minutes, or until mixture is batter-like in consistency and no flour is left on bottom of bowl. Cover with plastic wrap, rest sponge mixture in draft-free place for at least 4 hours (up to 12 hours).

2. Turn sponge mixture out on to floured surface, make well in centre, add plain flour, salt, extra yeast and about half the extra water to sponge mixture; knead dough. When dough has an elastic texture, add remaining extra water; knead 10 minutes. When dough is very soft, leave aside, uncovered, on the bench 10–15 minutes.

3. Transfer dough to floured surface, knead to collapse dough; place dough in large, oiled mixing bowl. Cover with plastic wrap; leave aside in warm place about 30 minutes.

4. To assemble flatbreads: Knock dough down on flat surface, transfer to floured surface. Work in more flour if necessary — the more flour, the easier dough is to work with. Leave aside, uncovered, on bench, 10 minutes.

5. Divide dough into four equal portions. Shape portions into 15-cm diameter circles with rolling pin or hands. Transfer to pizza or oven tray, work dough with fingers to edges; prick with fork through centre.

6. Divide onion topping and anchovies evenly among bases; place tray, preferably on terracotta tile, in preheated oven.

7. Bake 5–10 mins until golden brown. Rotate flatbread about halfway through time to cook evenly. Remove from oven; slice into small wedges and serve hot, sprinkled with salt, pepper, parsley and olive oil to taste.

Topping

Melt olive oil and butter in small frying pan; cook onion, stirring, about 10 minutes or until wilted and browned lightly. Add sugar and vinegar; cook, stirring, 3–5 minutes. Remove from heat, cool; adjust seasonings.

Ingredients *Makes 4 flatbread*

7 g fresh yeast
1 cup (250 ml) lukewarm water
1 cup (150 g) baker's flour
1²/₃ cups (250 g) plain flour
2 teaspoons salt
5 g fresh yeast, extra
³/₄ cup (180 ml) water, extra
¹/₄ cup plain flour (35 g), extra,
    for kneading

Topping

2 tablespoons olive oil
1 tablespoon butter
2 medium (300 g) brown onion,
    sliced thinly
1 tablespoon brown sugar
1–2 tablespoons (20–40 ml)
    balsamic vinegar
sea salt and black pepper,
    to taste
20–40g anchovy fillets
¹/₂ cup coarsely chopped flatleaf
    parsley
extra virgin olive oil for serving

Ballotine of ocean trout Peter Doyle

I wanted to showcase great Australian produce and this ballotine is a celebration of the fresh flavours that I believe define Australian cuisine. The recipe is a combination of refining a dish to suit our purposes at Celsius Restaurant and enhancing the fresh flavours of the ingredients.

Method

1. Remove the skin from the trout fillet and trim the brown flesh from the underside of the fillet. Cut the thinner belly section of the fillet to leave an even cylindrical shape the length of the fillet. Season with salt and cayenne pepper; cover with combined parsley, chervil, dill and chives, pressing down firmly into the fish.

2. Place the prepared fillet on 2 large pieces of plastic wrap; roll up very tightly to enhance the cylindrical shape. Tie at each end to form a large ballotine (this must be watertight to prevent any loss of fish juices).

3. Heat wide pan of water to 65°C, submerge fish, return to 65°C, cook 2 minutes. Remove pan from heat, allow to cool, leaving ballotine in the water. When cool, refrigerate overnight.

4. Slice ballotine, with plastic wrap still on, into rounds approximately 2 cm thick each weighing about 120 g. Remove plastic wrap.

5. Combine lemon juice and olive oil in screwtop jar to make lemon vinaigrette. Mix cucumber, half the extra chopped chives and 2 table-spoons lemon vinaigrette together in medium bowl; season with salt and pepper, divide among serving plates.

6. Mix crabmeat with ocean trout roe (reserve some for garnish), chilli, remaining chopped chives, 2 tablespoons lemon vinaigrette, salt and pepper. Divide crab mixture into 10 evenly-sized portions and arrange on top of cucumber salad. Place an ocean trout slice on top of the crabmeat, top with a little reserved ocean trout roe.

7. Decorate plates with land cress and a quenelle of acidulated cream, drizzle with remaining lemon vinaigrette.

Cream quenelles

Whip cream and lemon juice in small bowl until almost stiff, stir in dill; refrigerate until required. Just before serving, make quenelles by scoop-ing out a mound of cream with one tablespoon and using another to smooth it into an oval shape.

Chef's tip

Ensure ballotine is tightly wrapped in the 2 or 3 layers of plastic wrap and tied tightly to prevent water coming in contact with the trout during the poaching process.

Ingredients Serves 10

1.5 kg ocean trout fillet, skinned
salt and cayenne pepper, to taste
1/4 cup finely chopped flatleaf parsley
1/4 cup finely chopped chervil
1/4 cup finely chopped dill
1/4 cup finely chopped chives
2 1/2 tablespoons lemon juice
1 cup (250 ml) extra virgin olive oil
1 medium cucumber (170 g) seeded, sliced thinly
1 bunch chives, chopped finely, extra
salt and black pepper, to taste
250 g white spanner crabmeat
100 g ocean trout roe
2 serrano chillies, chopped finely
land cress, to serve

Cream quenelles

3/4 cup (180 ml) double cream
3 teaspoons lemon juice
1/2 bunch dill, chopped finely

Tuna spaghetti with anchovy breadcrumbs Anneka Manning

The best food is simple food done well, relying on sound basics, simple techniques and good ingredients. This recipe is fresh and uncomplicated — the hallmarks of how we eat today. It is perfect accompanied by a simple rocket and Parmesan salad dressed with a light red wine vinegar and extra virgin olive oil dressing.

Method

1. Cook spaghetti in a large saucepan of salted boiling water, uncovered, until just tender; drain. Return to pan; cover to keep warm.

2. Meanwhile, heat 2 tablespoons of the oil in large non-stick frying pan over medium heat; add anchovies, cook, stirring frequently, 1 minute or until anchovies break down. Add breadcrumbs and cook, stirring frequently, 3 minutes or until golden and crisp. Transfer breadcrumb mixture to plate and leave aside.

3. Wipe pan with paper towel; add 1 tablespoon of the remaining oil and heat over medium-high heat. Add tuna; cook 2–3 minutes each side until almost cooked through (or cooked as desired — the tuna will continue to cook on standing). Transfer to a plate and cover loosely with aluminium foil.

4. Using a zester, remove zest from two of the lemons. (Or, use a vegetable peeler to peel zest and small, sharp knife to remove white pith, then cut zest into very thin strips.) Juice lemons.

5. Combine remaining 1/2 cup (125 ml) oil with lemon zest, juice, green onion, garlic, parsley, basil, salt and pepper in large bowl. Add drained spaghetti and toss well to combine.

6. Break tuna into bite-sized chunks, add to pasta and toss gently to distribute evenly. Serve warm or at room temperature, sprinkled with anchovy breadcrumbs.

Ingredients Serves 6

500 g thin spaghetti

3/4 cup (180 ml) extra virgin olive oil

8 drained anchovy fillets, chopped

1 cup (70 g) fresh white breadcrumbs (made from Italian-style bread if possible)

600 g tuna steaks (each about 2.5 cm thick)

3 lemons

1 bunch green onions, trimmed, sliced thinly

2 large cloves garlic, chopped finely

1/2 cup finely chopped flatleaf parsley

1/2 cup finely chopped basil

1 teaspoon salt

black pepper, to taste

Coriander magic Jan Oldham

Commonly known by the totally unglamorous name of Green Gunge here in the west, this recipe is an SOS sanity saver and essential in my fridge.

The aromatic green paste originated very early in my voyage into the delights of all things Thai, before any such restaurants had opened in Perth. It's a much simplified variation of Thai green curry paste, created with what I just happened to have hanging around in the fridge at the time.

What makes it so sensational is that it's a wondrous way to make fresh coriander last a few weeks, while it's also a combination of all my favourite other culinary essentials like ginger, garlic, lemon and Thai fish sauce. Sometimes it has a fresh red chilli or two, sometimes they stay out and it's kept simple and zingy. I've made it with fresh basil instead of fresh coriander, sometimes used both, also adding a few sprigs of Vietnamese mint and precious Thai purple basil if they're hanging around.

Method

1. Wash coriander or basil thoroughly, rubbing off sandy grit from coriander roots. Don't bother to shake off excess water from leaves. Remove coriander leaves from stems and reserve leaves. Chop stems and roots coarsely. If using basil, remove leaves and discard stems (the stems have little flavour).

2. Combine coriander stem and root with lemon zest, garlic, ginger, chilli and lemongrass in bowl of food processor, process into very fine pieces.

3. Add basil or coriander leaves, lemon juice and fish sauce and process to combine. Store in a screw top jar in the fridge.

Chef's tips

• No one flavour should dominate — usually you use about equal quantities of juice and fish sauce — it really depends on how sour and juicy the lemons are, add more or less to taste.

• When storing in the fridge you can top the paste with olive oil. However, it doesn't seem to be essential and oil makes it less diet friendly.

• A few teaspoons transform almost any vegetable — heaven tossed over chunks of sweet potato or pumpkin, especially when combined with the crunch of lightly steamed snow peas. Try tossing new potatoes in a mixture of a few tablespoonfuls combined with about 1/2 cup natural yoghurt, sour cream or mayonnaise. Brushed over fish, chicken, lamb fillet or pork before grilling, frying or roasting, it's an easy and yummy marinade.

Ingredients

1 bunch coriander or basil
thinly peeled zest and juice
  1 lemon
2–4 cloves garlic, crushed
2.5cm piece fresh ginger,
  chopped coarsely
1 small red chilli, chopped
  coarsely (seeds optional)
1 stick lemongrass, white part
  only, chopped coarsely
2–3 tablespoons fish sauce.

Slow-cooked chicken Anders Ousback

This dish seems a lot of mucking about but it is really very easy and worth the convenience of the preparation. The cooking is somewhere between slow braising and gentle steaming, which perfumes the chicken and keeps it succulent: the texture is wonderful. The chicken evolves as a complete dish needing little more than a salad to accompany.

Method

1. Wash chicken; pat dry with paper towel. Mix all marinade ingredients together and combine with chicken in an oven bag. Tie bag closed; refrigerate at least 12 hours, turning occasionally. Remove chicken from oven bag; discard marinade.

2. To make stuffing: Place mushrooms in small heatproof bowl, cover with boiling water, stand 20 minutes; drain, squeeze out excess moisture, slice thinly. Grill sausage until half cooked; cut into 2 cm pieces. Heat oil in small frying pan, cook onion over low heat until transparent. Combine mushroom, sausage, onion, rice and Sichuan pepper in medium bowl; transfer mixture to chicken cavity, secure opening with skewer.

3. Soak lotus leaves in cold water for a few minutes, then wrap chicken in drained leaves. Tie chicken with kitchen string. Place chicken in oven bag, seal.

4. Place in cold oven, turn oven to slow (150°C); bake chicken 3½–4 hours. Switch off oven, rest 1 hour. Serve warm, simply carved with the stuffing.

Chef's tip

When slow cooking this dish a fan-forced oven can dramatically affect the cooking time. It is recommended that you reduce the oven temperature by at least 20°C if you are using a fan-forced oven unless the fan can be turned off during cooking.

Ingredients Serves 6

1.6–1.8 kg free-range chicken
2 dried lotus leaves

Marinade

⅔ cup (160 ml) sake
3 cm piece fresh ginger, sliced thinly
2 whole red chillies, chopped finely
2 cloves of garlic, sliced thinly
1 teaspoon sesame oil
sea salt, to taste

Stuffing

20 g dried shiitake mushrooms
350 g coarse pork sausage
2 tablespoons peanut oil
1 large onion (200 g), chopped finely
1 cup steamed sticky rice
Sichuan pepper, to taste

Salmon with caramelised onion and tomato Christine Salins

Farmed Atlantic salmon is one of the Australian food industry's greatest success stories of the past few decades. Grown in the pristine waters of Tasmania, it is expensive but because it's so rich, only small portions are needed. The following method cooks salmon fillets beautifully.

Method *Preheat oven to hot (220°–230°C).*

1. Heat oil in large ovenproof frying pan, cook salmon skin-side up 2 minutes, place salmon in pan in preheated oven; roast 6 minutes.
2. Divide bean purée evenly among six plates. Place a salmon fillet on each, and serve with a dollop of caramelised onion and tomato. Scatter baby spinach leaves alongside.

Caramelised onion and tomato

1. Heat oil in medium saucepan, add onion and cook, stirring frequently, over low heat about 10 minutes, or until onion is soft and golden.
2. Add vinegar and sugar and cook, stirring, until sugar dissolves. Add tomato and simmer, uncovered, 25–30 minutes until the mixture reduces and thickens. Leave aside, covered, until serving time.

White bean purée

1. Place beans in saucepan, cover with water; bring to a boil. Reduce heat; simmer, uncovered, 5 minutes. Drain.
2. Blend or process beans with olive oil and garlic until smooth. Season with salt and pepper. Leave aside, covered, until serving time.

Ingredients *Serves 6*

1 tablespoon olive oil
6 x 160–180 g fillets salmon or
  ocean trout
baby spinach leaves, to serve

Caramelised onion and tomato

1½ tablespoons extra-virgin
  olive oil
3 medium onions (450 g),
  sliced thinly
2 tablespoons raspberry or
  cherry vinegar
¼ cup (55 g) sugar
6 large tomatoes (1.5 kg),
  chopped coarsely

White bean purée

3 x 300 g cans butter beans,
  drained
⅓ cup (80 ml) olive oil
3 cloves garlic, crushed
salt and pepper, to taste

Smoked trout patties with lime sauce Barbara Northwood

I always loved the old-fashioned salmon patties my mother made using canned salmon and mashed potatoes. Through the years, the recipe developed into the one I have created using smoked trout. They are quick and easy to make and everyone loves them. Smoked salmon can be substituted for the trout and the amount of lime juice depends on personal taste. The patties can be made up to several hours ahead. Keep them covered, in the refrigerator, and fry just before serving.

Method

1. Boil, steam or microwave potato until tender. Drain well. Place in a large bowl, mash adding a little milk, if necessary, to achieve a smooth consistency. Add flaked trout, dill, zest, juice, green onion and tapenade; mix well.

2. Shape mixture into six evenly sized patties. Dip patties in beaten egg; coat in breadcrumbs. Place on tray; cover and refrigerate until required.

3. Heat oil in medium frying pan, shallow-fry patties until golden brown both sides and heated through. Drain on paper towel. Serve warm with lime sauce and herbs.

Lime sauce

Combine all ingredients in a small bowl; mix well.

Ingredients Makes 6

2 large potatoes (500 g), chopped coarsely
150 g smoked ocean trout with native blackening spice
1 tablespoon finely chopped dill
1 teaspoon finely grated lime zest
1 tablespoon lime juice
3 green onions, chopped finely
1 tablespoon green olive tapenade
1 egg, beaten lightly
1 cup (100 g) packaged breadcrumbs
oil for shallow frying
herbs, to garnish

Lime sauce

1/2 cup (140 g) Greek-style yoghurt
1/2 cup (150 g) mayonnaise
1 tablespoon lime juice
salt and pepper, to taste

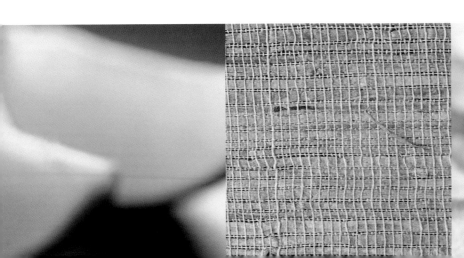

Stir-fried crayfish with chilli and black beans Margaret Johnson

This recipe came about because I am in the happy situation of having easy access to lots of crayfish, also known as the western rock lobster. Being such a rich meat, I prefer it cooked with powerful, clean flavours like those below. The inclusion of the shell not only helps hold the meat together nicely but when it is stir-fried it imparts a wonderful flavour to the meat. Enjoy it either as part of a shared meal or as a very indulgent dish, best served with plenty of rice to sop up those rich juices.

Method

1. Remove tails from crayfish, reserving the legs for a later snack. Remove the intestinal tract. Cut each tail, shell and all, into four or five medallions, with a cleaver.

2. Heat oil in wok; add garlic, lemongrass, ginger, coriander root and shallot, cook over moderate heat until shallot is transparent. You may need to add a little water to prevent the mixture burning. Add chillies and black beans, stir to combine. Increase heat to high, add cray sections, stir-fry several minutes, or until each section is covered with the mixture and shells have changed colour.

3. Add soy sauce, stir, cover wok; cook 5 minutes, stirring once. Check that the cray sections are cooked through; then stir in lime juice and coriander leaves. Serve with steamed jasmine rice.

Ingredients *Serves 4*

4 uncooked crayfish
1 tablespoon vegetable oil
1 tablespoon finely chopped garlic
1 stick lemongrass, white part only, chopped finely
1 tablespoon finely chopped fresh ginger
4 coriander roots, rinsed, chopped finely
5 shallots, sliced thinly
2–4 small red chillies
1 tablespoon black beans, mashed
1 tablespoon soy sauce
juice of 2 limes
1/4 cup loosely packed coriander leaves
steamed jasmine rice, to serve

Five-spice chicken with lentils Ian Parmenter

Five-spice marinated chicken pieces are browned then braised with vegetables and lentils. I find the green Puy lentils best, but you could also use brown lentils. Use chicken drumsticks or thigh cutlets or a combination of the two. Best to use a real, homemade chicken stock for this dish. The chicken can be marinated overnight and the dish made well in advance (up to three days) and reheated just before serving time.

Method *Preheat oven to moderate (180°C fan-forced).*

1. Mix soy sauce, sesame oil and five-spice powder in large bowl, add chicken, toss well to coat in marinade, cover; refrigerate 1 hour. Drain chicken; discard marinade.

2. Heat oil in large frying pan or wok (preferably non-stick). Cook chicken pieces until browned all over, about 6–7 minutes. Remove chicken from pan, leave aside.

3. Cook parsnip pieces over medium heat until browned all over, about 2–3 minutes; remove from pan, leave aside.

4. Cook onion, carrot and garlic, stirring occasionally, about 5 minutes. Add stock, lentils, pepper, orange rind (if using); bring to a boil.

5. Transfer lentil mixture to casserole dish. Add parsnip pieces, and place chicken pieces (they should not be covered with lentil mixture) on top. Cover. Bake in preheated oven approximately 1 hour, or until chicken is cooked through. Check halfway through cooking. If mixture looks too dry, add more stock.

6. Sprinkle with parsley and serve with creamy mashed potatoes or rice, and green vegetables.

Ingredients *Serves 6*

1 tablespoon dark soy sauce
1 tablespoon sesame oil
$1/2$ teaspoon five-spice powder
12 chicken pieces
1 tablespoon peanut oil
2 medium parsnips (250 g), cut into long wedges
1 medium onion (150 g), chopped coarsely
2 medium carrots (240 g), chopped finely
2–3 cloves garlic, crushed
3 cups (750 ml) chicken stock
100 g green lentils, washed and drained
$1/4$ teaspoon white pepper
1 strip orange rind (optional)
2 tablespoons finely chopped flatleaf parsley

Barramundi poached in coconut milk Neil Perry

At Rockpool, the fish is cooked in a copper pot, in which it is served at the table. When the lid is lifted the perfume from the garam masala and sweet Thai basil is glorious. The fish and broth are spooned over a bed of semolina noodles and blanched snow peas. Red emperor, snapper and other reef fish make excellent substitutes. When we make garam masala in-house, each spice is dry-roasted separately then ground together. The spice mixture should be made in small amounts as, when it's stored, it loses its aroma.

Method

1. To make tomato and chilli base: Heat vegetable oil in medium heavy-based saucepan, add onion, garlic, turmeric, chilli, ginger and salt; cook slowly over low heat, stirring occasionally, 1 hour or until onion caramelises. Add tomato; cook, stirring occasionally, 10 minutes. Remove from heat, cover; leave aside until ready to use.
2. In a frying pan with a tight-fitting lid, large enough to hold the fish snugly, combine tomato and chilli base, coconut milk, lime leaves, ginger, garam masala, fish sauce and palm sugar. Bring to a boil. Add fish, presentation side up, and lower the heat to just under a boil. Cover with lid; cook very slowly over very low heat 8 minutes, making sure that the mixture never boils.
3. Remove pan from heat and rest, covered, 5 minutes. Add coconut cream and basil, and replace the lid. Place fish on a bed of semolina noodles with blanched snow peas and spoon broth over.

Garam masala

1. Crack roasted cardamom pods in a mortar and pestle and remove black seeds.
2. Combine seeds with remaining roasted spices, discard the husks and grind spice mixture in mortar and pestle or spice or coffee grinder to a fine powder.
3. Store in airtight container until required.

Garam masala

1½ tablespoons green
   cardamom pods, roasted
½ teaspoon cloves, roasted
½ teaspoon white peppercorns,
   roasted
1 cinnamon stick, roasted
2 star anise, roasted

Ingredients Serves 6

Tomato and chilli base

¼ cup (60 ml) vegetable oil
1 large brown onion (200 g),
   diced finely
3 cloves garlic, chopped finely
2 cm piece fresh turmeric,
   chopped finely
5 small green chillies, chopped
   finely
2 teaspoons finely chopped fresh
   ginger
sea salt, to taste
6 vine-ripened tomatoes, diced

For the fish

4 cups (1L) coconut milk
6 kaffir lime leaves, shredded
   finely
3 cm piece fresh ginger,
   shredded finely
1 teaspoon garam masala
1½ tablespoons fish sauce
⅓ cup (90 g) shaved palm sugar
1.5 kg whole barramundi, filleted,
   skinned, cut into 6 portions
2½ tablespoons coconut cream
leaves from ½ bunch Thai basil
semolina noodles and blanched
   snow peas, to serve

Crusted prawns with fennel and Persian feta salad Belinda Franks

This recipe has been selected because it is a very easy, fast dish to prepare when you are having guests. Everything except cooking the prawns can be done beforehand so you don't have to spend time in the kitchen instead of relaxing with your friends. The sweetness of the currants compliments the salty tang and richness of the Persian feta, while the aniseed flavour of fennel is in harmony with the prawns. If possible barbecue or grill the prawns for a smoky flavour. The salad goes equally well with salmon or ocean trout.

Method

1. Combine chilli, salt, lime zest, cumin, fennel and olive oil in large bowl; add prawns, toss to coat in spice mixture.
2. Cook prawns on heated oiled grill plate (or grill, barbecue or pan fry), a few minutes each side, or until prawns change colour.
3. Divide fennel salad among serving plates; top with cooked prawns. Sprinkle over crumbled feta and drizzle with combined dill, chives and extra olive oil.

Shaved fennel salad

Mix all ingredients together in large bowl.

Chef's tips

• The salad is best made at least 2 hours before needed.
• A Japanese grater or benriner is the ideal implement for shaving the fennel thinly.

Ingredients Serves 4

1 teaspoon finely chopped chilli
2 teaspoons sea salt
2 teaspoons finely grated
   lime zest
1 teaspoon roasted cumin seeds,
   crushed
1 teaspoon roasted fennel seeds,
   crushed
$1/4$ cup (60 ml) extra virgin olive oil
24 large uncooked prawns,
   shelled, deveined
120 g feta cheese, crumbled
2 tablespoons finely chopped dill
2 tablespoons finely chopped
   chives
$2 1/2$ tablespoons additional
   extra virgin olive oil

Shaved fennel salad

2 bulbs fennel (1 kg), shaved thinly
$3/4$ cup (105 g) currants
1 bunch mint, chopped coarsely
1 bunch flatleaf parsley, chopped
   coarsely
1 lime, cut into segments
2 tablespoons lime juice
2 tablespoons extra virgin olive oil
2–3 tablespoons chardonnay
   vinegar
sea salt and sugar, to taste

Thai green chicken curry Neale Whitaker

I'm a Brit — and a Thai food nut — and one of the things I love most about living in Australia is the availability of good, authentic south-east Asian food. The key to this dish is to throw in the vital ingredients — the kaffir lime leaves, the coconut milk, the coriander, lime juice and fish sauce — right at the last minute for a wonderful, aromatic flavour hit. And hunt down the little pea eggplants if you can, their texture makes all the difference.

Method

1. To make curry paste: place all the ingredients in a food processor or blender and whiz to a paste.
2. Trim chicken fillets; cut into 3-cm pieces. Heat oil in a large saucepan over medium heat, add green curry paste and cook 1–2 minutes, stirring to release the flavours.
3. Add chicken and eggplants, cook, stirring, about 6–8 minutes, or until chicken is almost cooked through.
4. Add lime leaves and coconut milk, reduce heat; simmer 2 minutes.
5. Just before serving, add lime juice, fish sauce and coriander. Serve with steamed jasmine rice.

Chef's tip
The green curry paste will keep for 2 weeks, covered, in the refrigerator.

Ingredients *Serves 4*

Green curry paste
6 long green chillies, seeded, chopped coarsely
2 small green chillies, seeded, chopped coarsely
6 shallots, chopped coarsely
1/4 cup finely chopped lemon grass, white part only
1/2 cup coarsely chopped coriander roots and leaves
1 tablespoon grated fresh ginger
1 tablespoon chopped garlic
1 tablespoon lime juice
1 tablespoon coarsely grated palm sugar
2 tablespoons peanut oil
1 teaspoon dried shrimp paste
1 teaspoon turmeric
1/2 teaspoon ground mace
2 teaspoons ground cumin
1 teaspoon ground coriander

Chicken curry
1 tablespoon peanut oil
green curry paste (see above)
1 kg chicken thigh fillets
150 g pea eggplants (optional)
4 kaffir lime leaves
3 cups (750 ml) coconut milk
2 tablespoons lime juice
1 1/2 tablespoons fish sauce
1/2 cup coriander leaves

Rosemary-scented lamb cutlets Jan Power

I grew up on a sheep property and I believed until I was five that the entire world lived entirely on sheep meat as happily as I did. Lamb in all shapes and flavours, celebrated by myriad recipes, covers the complete history of our country and kitchen fare. Lamb chops were served with parsley mash and frozen peas. We ate stewed neck chops in gravy with spuds and carrots on weeknights and had devilled lamb's kidney or lamb's fry and bacon for breakfast. Later on for dinner parties, we baked expensive racks with a herb crust and put silver foil socks decorated with red currant jelly blobs on the tips. Now we buy our fancy fatless cuts, quickly grill, simmer or barbecue them and anoint them with pestos and sauces.

Method

1. Place cutlets and rosemary in shallow baking dish. Add garlic, olive oil and verjuice, toss to coat; refrigerate overnight, turn cutlets several times. (If preparing for a picnic or barbecue, pack cutlets in a strong plastic box with lid.) Before cooking, drain, discard marinade and season the meat.

2. Cook cutlets on heated oiled grill plate (or grill or barbecue). Stand cutlets upright against each other and cover loosely with a few sheets of aluminium foil made into a little tent or lid. Cook cutlets 2 minutes each side. Remove from heat; leave aside, covered, to keep warm.

3. Toast pitta bread both sides. Arrange cutlets and pitta bread on serving plates. Serve with chutney, mint jelly or beetroot relish, and salads such as couscous and green pea, warm brown rice with burnt almonds, green herbs and rocket or hot chargrilled root vegetables with pine nuts.

Ingredients Serves 4–8

16 thick lamb cutlets

1 bunch rosemary

2 cloves garlic, sliced thinly

1/3 cup (80 ml) extra virgin olive oil

2 tablespoons verjuice, or good red wine vinegar

sea salt and lemon pepper, to taste

4–8 pieces pitta bread

chutney, mint jelly or beetroot relish, to serve

Chilli mango chicken with coriander noodles Brigid Treloar

This recipe is the result of particular interests (and the subject of some of my cookbooks) — healthy steaming, Asian flavours, eye-appealing sushi and easy preparation. The chicken is rolled around colourful and tasty fillings and wrapped in spinach leaves so when it is steamed and sliced it looks like sushi.

Method

1. Halve chicken fillets lengthways, cover with plastic wrap and pound gently with a meat mallet.

2. Combine chilli sauce, lime juice, ginger and garlic and brush over chicken slices.

3. Place 2 or 3 slices each of mango and capsicum and a piece of green onion at one end of chicken slice and roll up to enclose filling. Repeat with remaining chicken and fillings.

4. Place 2 or 3 spinach leaves on workbench, slightly overlapping; brush with remaining chilli sauce mixture. Place a chicken roll at one end and wrap spinach around to enclose chicken; secure with a toothpick. Repeat with remaining rolls. (This can be done ahead and chicken refrigerated until required.)

5. Place chicken in bamboo steamer, cover and place over wok or pot of rapidly simmering water, ensuring water does not touch base of steamer. Steam 10–12 minutes, or until chicken juices run clear when skewer is inserted in thickest part. Add rice noodles to simmering water for the last 4–5 minutes and cook until tender.

6. Remove steamer and leave covered 2–3 minutes while preparing noodles. Drain noodles. Heat coconut cream in wok, add noodles and toss to combine. Add soy sauce, coriander, lime juice and zest to taste.

7. Slice chicken or cut in half diagonally; serve on noodles.

Chef's tips

• Coconut cream is used to stop the noodles sticking together. Oil can be substituted, and somen or soba noodles can be substituted for rice noodles. Adjust cooking times.

• Tenderloins can also be made into small rolls for finger food.

• Chicken slices can be served as finger food on toothpicks with soy sauce for dipping.

Ingredients Makes 8 rolls

4 chicken breast fillets, tenderloin removed

1/3 cup (80 ml) sweet chilli sauce

1 teaspoon lime juice

1 teaspoon finely grated fresh ginger

1 small clove garlic, crushed

1 small mango (300 g), sliced (or use canned)

1 small red capsicum (150 g), seeds and membranes removed, sliced thinly

2 green onions, quartered

18–24 large English spinach leaves, blanched

300 g dried flat rice noodles

1/4 cup (60 ml) coconut cream

2 teaspoons salt-reduced soy sauce

2 tablespoons coarsely chopped coriander leaves

juice and zest of 1 lime

Mud crab tom yum Cherry Ripe

In 1988 I spent a wondrous week at the cooking school at the Mandarin Oriental Hotel in Bangkok, in hands-on classes learning the basics of Thai food under the legendary, charismatic teacher Chalie Amatyakul. Back then, many of the ingredients — fresh makrut (kaffir lime) leaves, fresh galangal, coriander roots — were hard to find here, but are much more widely available now. Although tom yum is more usually made with prawns, it adapts beautifully to mud crabs steamed in this hot-sour broth. For the broth it is perfectly acceptable to use tom yum paste (sold in jars and sachets) but I prefer to titivate it with fresh ingredients. You will need a very large, preferably heavy-based, stainless steel stockpot for this recipe.

Method

1. Clean crabs under running water, rubbing any mud or slime off the shells. Remove the innards (mustard) and gills (deadman's fingers), leaving only the translucent white flesh, legs and claws. Crack the large claws by hitting them with a mallet or back of a cleaver. Place crab segments into large stockpot with a lid.
2. Heat oil in large saucepan, fry garlic gently 1 minute. Add tom yum paste, the water, lime zest, juice and leaves, fish sauce, lemongrass, galangal, tamarind, chilli and coriander roots and bring to a boil. Reduce heat, simmer 5 minutes to allow flavours to infuse. Adjust seasonings — it should be hot (spicy) and sour.
3. Scoop out and discard some of the leaves, stalks and galangal; pour boiling broth over crab. Place over high heat; cover so that the pieces at the top, even if not submerged, will steam. Bring back to a boil; cook 5 minutes.
4. Turn crab so the pieces at the top go to the bottom and are immersed in the broth. Cover, cook 3 minutes, or until shells turn orange-red.
5. Remove from heat, sprinkle with coriander and green onion. Divide tom yum among large individual soup bowls, with soup spoons (for the broth) crab crackers and some robust bread.

Chef's tips

• Unless they're wearing bathers, provide guests with the biggest napkins you possess and tie them bib-like around the back of their necks. (They will thank you for what this saves them on dry cleaning bills!)
• Put large bowls in the centre of the table for empty shells and detritus, and a couple of large finger bowls of warm water with lemon slices for rinsing sticky fingers.
• Choose weighty crabs. The heavier they are for their body size, the meatier they will be. Ask the fishmonger to cut them into quarters.
• Tahitian limes are easier to zest than kaffir limes, if you haven't got a zester, use a vegetable peeler to remove zest (no pith) and finely chop.

Ingredients Serves 8

4 x 1 kg mud crabs, jointed
vegetable oil, for frying
3 cloves garlic, crushed
1 tablespoon tom yum paste (or more, to taste)
4 cups (1L) water
3 limes, zested and juiced
6 kaffir lime leaves, torn in half
1 tablespoon fish sauce
2 sticks of lemongrass, white part only, sliced thinly, diagonally
12 cm piece fresh galangal, sliced thinly
1 teaspoon tamarind pulp (optional, lime juice may provide sufficient acidity)
1 small chilli, sliced thinly (optional)
roots of 1 bunch coriander, chopped finely
leaves of 1 bunch coriander, chopped coarsely, for garnish
1 bunch green onions, chopped coarsely, for garnish

Roasted quail with pea mousseline Suzanne Gibbs

This is a delectable yet manageable dish for a special occasion. Serve it in the old-fashioned generous way on a large serving platter, brought to the table for guests to help themselves; or 'chic-modern' with individual plates made up, the purée in the centre and the quail jointed (halved or quartered with scissors) and arranged on top. The mousseline of green peas may be made ahead, the quail prepared ahead and ready for the oven. Think of offering finger bowls — fingers will be needed to eat the quail.

Method Preheat oven to hot (230°C).

1. Wipe quail with damp paper towel; season with salt and pepper. Put a small piece of orange zest and a sprig of thyme and parsley inside each quail. Tie birds into a neat shape with string.

2. Heat oil and butter in heavy flameproof casserole and brown the quail all over. Pour over verjuice; let it bubble for 30 seconds. Cover casserole and bake quail in preheated oven 15–20 minutes, basting several times during cooking with the juices. Remove from oven and rest until required. Reduce oven temperature to moderate (180°C).

3. To prepare pea mousseline: Combine peas in medium heavy-based saucepan with lettuce and butter. Cover and cook over gentle heat until tender, shaking the pan occasionally. Remove from heat, season with salt and pepper; purée in mouli or food processor. Return to saucepan, add cream and heat gently. This may be done ahead and reheated just before serving.

4. Spoon pea mousseline on to an ovenproof serving platter. Remove the strings from quail and arrange birds on the purée. Return to oven for 10 minutes.

Ingredients Serves 6–8

6–8 quail
salt and black pepper, to taste
2 strips orange zest, pared thinly
fresh thyme and parsley sprigs
2 tablespoons olive oil
60 g butter
1/2 cup (125 ml) verjuice

Green pea mousseline

500 g shelled green peas, fresh
  or frozen
1/2 iceberg lettuce, shredded finely
60 g butter
salt and black pepper, to taste
1/2 cup (125 ml) cream

Mustard seed lamb Elise Pascoe

This recipe was devised to illustrate the versatility of Fresh Australian Range Lamb for the North American market, for which I spearheaded the recipe development for the Australian Meat & Livestock Corporation for 10 years. It has stood the test of time as it is both delicious and easy to prepare.

Method

1. Heat a heavy frying pan, large enough to hold fillets in a single layer, over medium/high heat. When hot, add butter and oil.

2. Season lamb, add to pan, brown all sides, 6–8 minutes depending on size of back straps.

3. When lamb is cooked as desired, remove to a warm plate, cover loosely with aluminium foil to keep warm while resting.

4. Discard fat from pan juices; return pan to medium/high heat. Add wine, whisk to incorporate caramelised juices. Add mustard and cream and stir until combined. Simmer until sauce thickens slightly; adjust seasonings.

5. Slice the rested lamb; add juices to the sauce. Pour some sauce on each plate and serve sliced lamb on top.

Ingredients *Serves 6*

45 g unsalted butter
1 tablespoon olive oil
salt and black pepper, to taste
6 x 200 g lamb backstraps, silver
  skins removed
1/4 cup (60 ml) dry red wine
3 tablespoons seed mustard
1 cup (250 ml) cream

Pride of Andalucia Margaret Fulton

A beautiful dessert cake from the land of good oranges. An old, old recipe that changed hands at Oxford University between two visiting caring academic cooks — it is rightly known as the Pride of Andalucia as it showcases the juicy oranges and creamy almonds from that part of Spain.

Method *Preheat oven to moderately slow (150°C).*

1. Grease 20-cm-round cake pan; line base with non-stick baking paper. Sprinkle the 5 teaspoons caster sugar as evenly as possible over base of pan. Slice unpeeled oranges as thinly as possible, removing any pips. Leave aside.

2. Cream butter in medium bowl with electric mixer; beat in extra sugar gradually. Beat in eggs, one at a time, until thoroughly incorporated. Sift flour with salt and fold into the creamed mixture with ground almonds.

3. Arrange just over a third of the orange slices (the best ones) over caster sugar in pan, overlapping them quite a bit. Spread a thin layer, about a third, of cake mixture on top. Arrange another layer of orange slices over mixture. Spread half the remaining cake mixture over, then the last of the orange slices. Finish with remaining cake mixture.

4. Bake cake in centre of preheated oven for about 2 hours until the top is dark brown.

5. Remove from oven, cool a few minutes; ease sides of the cake with a metal spatula. Invert the cake on to a serving plate and leave to cool.

6. Heat marmalade or jam with the water in small saucepan, stirring until smooth. Leaving the shreds behind, brush the glaze over the top of cake, but not down the sides. Leave to cool completely and serve with dollops of thick cream.

Ingredients *Serves 8*

5 teaspoons caster sugar

3 medium oranges (720 g)

175 g unsalted butter

$3/4$ cup (165 g) caster sugar, extra

3 large eggs

$1/2$ cup (75 g) self-raising flour

$1/2$ teaspoon salt

$1^1/4$ cups (155 g) ground almonds

$1/3$ cup (110 g) orange jam (or golden shred marmalade)

2 teaspoons water

Mango and berry trifle Gabriel Gaté

I created this luscious trifle for a Christmas lunch. The mango can be replaced by juicy peaches, and the berries by seeded cherries. Serve the trifle in a large glass bowl or individual parfait glasses. Take care not to overbeat when you're mixing in the mascarpone, or you could end up with butter.

Method

1. Whisk egg yolks with 2 tablespoons of the caster sugar in small bowl with electric mixer until creamy. Mix in mascarpone; fold in cream.
2. Beat egg whites in small bowl with electric mixer until stiff peaks form; beat in remaining sugar. Fold this mixture gently through the mascarpone mixture; fold in hazelnuts.
3. Scoop passionfruit pulp into small bowl. Prepare berries, wash and hull strawberries.
4. Arrange alternating layers of sponge finger biscuits, fruit and mascarpone mixture in glass serving bowl. Feel free to change the order of the layers, but it's a good idea to finish with a layer of mascarpone mixture. Refrigerate, covered with plastic wrap, several hours or overnight.
5. Decorate top with extra fruit. Dust with icing sugar just before serving.

Ingredients Serves 8–10

2 eggs, separated
$1/3$ cup (75 g) caster sugar
250 g mascarpone cheese
300 ml cream, whipped
$2/3$ cup (100 g) roasted hazelnuts, chopped coarsely
4 passionfruit
500 g mixed berries (raspberries, blueberries, strawberries)
2 large mangoes, sliced thinly
12 sponge finger biscuits, halved lengthways
extra fruit, for decoration
icing sugar, for dusting

The ultimate chocolate cake Joanna Savill

When Maeve O'Meara and I published our first cookbook (*Lamingtons and Lemongrass*, Allen & Unwin) in 1998, we were given a fabulous chocolate cake recipe by our friend, journalist and broadcaster Vivian Schenker. It came from her grandmother, Mitzi Kuhn, who owned one of Sydney's first 'continental' cake shops. I've since played around with it a little in my search for the ultimate cake — and I think I've found it.

Method *Preheat oven to moderate (180°C).*

1. Grease and line 20-cm-round springform cake pan.

2. Combine butter and caster sugar in bowl, beat with electric mixer until light and fluffy.

3. Add egg yolks, one at a time, to the creamed butter and sugar, beating well between additions.

4. Beat egg whites with salt in small bowl with electric mixer about 2 minutes, or until stiff peaks form.

5. Stir cooled chocolate and vanilla into the creamed mixture; fold in flour and ground hazelnuts.

6. Fold in a quarter of the beaten egg white and mix to combine. Add remaining egg white, folding through gently until combined.

7. Spoon mixture into prepared pan; bake in preheated oven about 50 minutes, or until cake is springy to touch.

8. Stand cake in pan 10 minutes; turn out on to wire rack. Dust with sifted icing sugar and enjoy — preferably while still warm.

Ingredients *Serves 8–10*

180 g butter, softened

$^3/_4$ cup (165 g) caster sugar

4 eggs, separated

pinch salt

125 g bittersweet chocolate, melted and cooled

few drops vanilla extract

$^2/_3$ cup (100 g) self-raising flour, sifted

$^1/_2$ cup (55 g) ground roasted hazelnuts

icing sugar, for dusting

Iced chocolate fruit pudding Annette Forrest

I love serving indulgent desserts that can be made in advance — this one is my absolute favourite. My family and friends love it too! Use good-quality fruits and the best Belgian chocolate. Leave the fruit to soak overnight, if possible. At Christmas, I add 50 g chopped angelica and substitute the amaretto with rum.

Method

1. Place cherries, raisins, sultanas, pineapple, prunes and amaretto in medium bowl. Stir to combine; leave aside, 1 hour, stirring occasionally.
2. Combine chocolate and 1 cup (250 ml) of the cream in medium heatproof bowl; place bowl over saucepan of simmering water (make sure bowl does not touch water) and melt chocolate gently, stirring occasionally, until smooth and well combined. Remove bowl from heat; leave mixture aside to cool slightly.
3. Combine egg yolks and sugar in large heatproof mixing bowl; beat mixture with electric mixer until thick and pale. Add cooled chocolate mixture, beat until well combined.
4. Place bowl over saucepan of simmering water; beat 5 minutes, or until mixture is thick and mousse-like. Remove bowl from heat; leave aside to cool.
5. Place the remaining 1 cup (250 ml) cream in small bowl and whip with electric mixer until soft peaks form. Fold cream through cooled chocolate mixture with a large metal spoon. Add fruit (and any remaining liqueur) and hazelnuts, stir gently to combine.
6. Spoon mixture into a 8-cup (2-L) pudding bowl. Cover with aluminium foil and freeze 8–10 hours, or until firm. Slice and serve.

Ingredients Serves 8–10

¾ cup (150 g) glace cherries, halved
½ cup (85 g) raisins
½ cup (80 g) sultanas
approx 4 rings (100 g) glace pineapple, chopped coarsely
⅔ cup (100 g) plump seeded prunes, chopped coarsely
⅓ cup (80 ml) amaretto liqueur
200 g dark chocolate, chopped coarsely
2 cups (500 ml) thickened cream
4 egg yolks
⅓ cup (75 g) caster sugar
½ cup (75 g) roasted hazelnuts, chopped coarsely

Roast hazelnut brownies Janelle Bloom

Cakes and slices don't traditionally convert well to microwave cooking, however this recipe is better in the microwave. It's moist, rich and chewy and best of all, only takes 24 minutes to cook. If you would like to serve it warm, heat one slice, uncovered, 30 seconds on medium-low/defrost/30% power.

Method

1. Grease base of 18-cm square heatproof, microwave-safe container; line with non-stick baking paper.
2. Place hazelnuts in oven bag, twist the bag to secure. Cook on High/100% power, 4–5 minutes, or until nuts are roasted, shaking the bag gently every minute. Wrap hazelnuts in a clean tea towel and rub to remove as much skin as possible. Chop hazelnuts coarsely.
3. Cream butter, sugar and vanilla in medium bowl with electric mixer until well combined (do not over mix, it does not need to be light and fluffy). Add eggs one at a time, mixing with a spoon.
4. Place chocolate in clean dry microwave-safe bowl. Heat, uncovered, 2–3 minutes on medium/50% power, stirring every minute with a metal spoon. Add chocolate to butter mixture; stir to combine.
5. Fold flour and three quarters of the chopped hazelnuts into chocolate mixture. Spread into prepared dish. Place on microwave-safe rack, 2 cm above turntable (alternatively, turn a dinner plate upside down); cook, uncovered, on medium/50% power 9–10 minutes (the top should still be slightly sticky).
6. Scatter remaining hazelnuts over top; cook, uncovered, 4–6 minutes on medium/50% power (the centre should still be a little moist). Allow to stand, uncovered, in dish until cooled to room temperature.
7. Cut into squares; dust with cocoa powder or icing sugar if desired. Serve with thick cream or ice-cream.

Ingredients *Makes 16 pieces*

1$\frac{1}{3}$ cups (200 g) hazelnuts
125 g butter
1$\frac{1}{2}$ cups (330 g) brown sugar
1 teaspoon vanilla extract
3 eggs
200 g dark chocolate, chopped coarsely
$\frac{3}{4}$ cup (110 g) plain flour, sifted
cocoa powder or icing sugar, for dusting
thick cream or ice-cream, to serve

Spiced pistachio honey bites Kay Francis

I devised this concoction of some of my favourite things to be included in a picnic menu for my new book, *Travelling Food* (New Holland, 2002). The bites keep very well, refrigerated in a covered container, for two weeks, although you will probably have to hide them in the back of the fridge! If only using a small portion, keep remainder uncut until required. It is more economical to buy this quantity of pistachios at a specialist Middle Eastern food shop.

Method *Preheat oven to moderate (180°C).*

1. Brush each sheet of filo with some of the butter (you should have ½ cup (125 ml) left for the recipe). Lay filo in a 27 x 17.5 x 3 cm baking dish, to cover base only.

2. Combine remaining ingredients (except extra pistachios) in large mixing bowl; stir until thoroughly combined.

3. Spoon into baking dish on top of filo; press down until mixture is firmly packed. Cut each extra kernel in half lengthways; arrange, cut side up, in a decorative pattern on top of mixture, pressing down on each piece firmly to secure.

4. Place dish in centre of preheated oven and bake 20–25 minutes (if mixture begins to bubble up at edges, reduce oven temperature to 160°C for last 5 minutes). Cool in dish; cut into small bites.

Ingredients *Makes about 40*

4 sheets filo pastry

150 g butter, melted

4 cups (600 g) pistachio kernels, chopped coarsely

1 cup (220 g) firmly packed dark brown sugar

1 tablespoon ground cinnamon

1 teaspoon freshly grated nutmeg

1 tablespoon ground cardamom

½ cup (180 g) honey

1 tablespoon rosewater

½ cup (75 g) pistachio kernels, extra, for decoration

tomorrow

'The future heralds a return to flavour, rejecting diets, fads and artificially created food, and, learning from our multicultural society, valuing taking time to eat, and doing so without guilt.'
Lyndey Milan

Black pepper chicken tea Christine Manfield

This is a classic consommé soup, using Asian flavours and technique and playing with the concept of a cup of tea. It has the appearance and colour of black tea; tea is used in the preparation of the chicken to impart flavour. It was a regular feature on our later menus at Paramount and remains a constant in my repertoire.

Method Preheat oven to moderate (180°C).

1. Make the spice salt by dry roasting the salt and peppercorns toge-ther in a cast iron pan over very low heat for a few minutes. Cool; grind in a spice grinder until powdered.

2. Rub a teaspoon of the spice salt on to the surface of the chicken breast; reserve remaining spice salt.

3. Combine remaining ingredients for tea smoking mixture. Line wok with aluminium foil and heat over high flame. Add tea smoking mixture and when it starts to smoke (about 30 seconds), sit a wire rack with the chicken breast on it in the wok. Cover with tight-fitting lid; wrap wet tea towel around lid to prevent smoke escaping.

4. Smoke over high heat for 8 minutes; turn the chicken over, smoke 6 minutes or until chicken is just cooked. The surfaces take on a brown hue as the tea tannins are imparted during the smoking process.

5. Remove chicken and leave aside to cool. Carefully wrap burnt leftovers in the foil and cool before discarding.

6. To make the tea: roast garlic wrapped in aluminium foil, in preheated oven 30 minutes or until soft. Cool, slice thickly.

7. Heat oil in heavy-based stockpot; fry onion, chilli and ginger until onion softens and begins to colour. Add peppercorns; deglaze pan with rice wine. Remove pan from heat when wine comes to a boil.

8. Add roasted garlic, lime leaves, green onion, chicken stock and soy sauce to stockpot and bring slowly to a boil over gentle heat. Reduce heat, simmer 1 hour, skimming surface regularly with mesh spoon. Do not boil further or consommé (tea) will become cloudy.

Ingredients Serves 6

Spice salt

1 teaspoon sea salt

1 teaspoon Sichuan peppercorns

Tea-smoked chicken

1 x 300 g free-range chicken breast

2 teaspoons oolong tea leaves

1 teaspoon jasmine tea leaves

1 piece dried tangerine peel

$1/2$ teaspoon finely grated orange zest

2 teaspoons jasmine rice

2 teaspoons brown sugar

1 star anise

$1/2$ teaspoon Sichuan peppercorns

1 piece cassia bark, broken into small pieces

Chicken tea

1 head garlic

1 tablespoon vegetable oil

1 medium brown onion (150 g),
    chopped

1 large red chilli, sliced thinly

1 teaspoon finely chopped fresh
    ginger

$1/2$ teaspoon black peppercorns,
    cracked

1 teaspoon Sichuan peppercorns,
    cracked

10 teaspoons (50 ml) Chinese
    rice wine (shaoxing)

3 kaffir lime leaves, shredded
    finely

3 green onions, chopped finely

8 cups (2 L) chicken stock

10 teaspoons (50 ml) light
    Chinese soy sauce

6 teaspoons (30 ml) fish sauce

5 teaspoons (25 ml) lime juice,
    strained

$1/2$ punnet (50 g) enoki
    mushrooms, trimmed

12 chives, chopped finely

$1/2$ cup tiny watercress leaves

2 tablespoons coriander leaves

9. Strain consommé through muslin-lined sieve or a jelly bag to ensure stock is clear and free of sediment; press to extract as much liquid as possible. Discard solids, cool liquid; refrigerate, covered. Remove any fat before using.

10. Strain cooled consommé into clean saucepan, avoiding any sediment. Bring to a simmer; add fish sauce and lime juice, cook 3 minutes. Adjust seasonings if necessary.

11. To serve, shred smoked chicken and sprinkle with remaining spice salt. Divide chicken and remaining ingredients among cups, then ladle in hot consommé and swirl with a chopstick to combine.

Chef's tips

- To serve as a taste, use fine porcelain espresso cups and saucers.
- To serve as an entrée, use Chinese-style rice/soup bowls.

Garfish nigiri-zushi Hideo Dekura

When I arrived in Sydney in 1972, sushi was hardly known in Australia. How times have changed! You must use short grain rice, and of all those available in Australia, I have found that Koshihikari is the closest to the Japanese type. Grown in Leeton, NSW, it has a gentle aroma and retains some moisture after cooking, which is important for sushi. Wasabi is the tangy green additive sometimes known as Japanese mustard because of its pungency. The taste is very strong, so you only need a dot. It should not dominate the sushi flavour.

Method

1. Rinse rice thoroughly in large bowl of cold water, using palm of hand to press rice. Drain; repeat three times. Continue to run cold water over rice in strainer until water runs clear. Leave rice in strainer 30 minutes.

2. Place drained rice, the water and mirin or sake, if desired, in medium saucepan, cover tightly; bring to a boil. Reduce heat, simmer, covered, about 12 minutes or until water is absorbed. Remove from heat, stand, covered, 20 minutes. Meanwhile, combine rice vinegar, salt and sugar in small bowl; stir until sugar dissolves.

3. Moisten a cloth lightly with vinegar/water mixture; wipe inside of flat-bottomed bowl or tray. Using moistened rice paddle, place rice in bowl. With moistened paddle, add vinegar/sugar mixture to rice gradually using a cutting action to lift and separate the grains. Continue this process, while fanning mixture with a hand-held or low-speed electric fan to cool rice as it absorbs vinegar mixture. This helps to make rice shiny and enhance its taste.

4. Cover rice with damp cloth, stand at room temperature until ready to use. Do not refrigerate, as this causes rice to lose stickiness and harden. Rice can be prepared an hour or so before it is required, but sushi should be assembled immediately prior to serving.

5. Rub sea salt into fingers to prevent slipping; skin fillets by pulling skin in a single motion towards tail. Use a sharp knife to score along dark line on each fillet to show colour of fish and improve malleability.

6. To make nigiri-zushi (hand-moulded sushi): Lightly moisten hands, roll 1-tablespoon measures of sushi rice into tall 2-cm rounds. Wrap a garfish fillet around each rice round and leave aside.

7. Place dot of wasabi on sushi and top with sieved egg and pinch of mustard cress.

8. Place two pieces of sushi on each plate and serve with pickled ginger and soy sauce in separate bowls.

Ingredients Serves 4

1 cup (200 g) Koshihikari rice
1 cup (250 ml) water
2 teaspoons mirin or sake, optional
2 tablespoons rice vinegar
pinch sea salt
1 tablespoon caster sugar
medium bowl filled with water and rice vinegar mixed in a ratio of 1 part vinegar to 10 parts water, for moistening implements
8 x 60 g sashimi-quality garfish, filleted
2 teaspoons wasabi paste or 2 teaspoons wasabi powder mixed with 3 teaspoons water
2 hard-boiled egg yolks, sieved
1 tablespoon mustard cress
1/4 cup (50 g) pickled ginger (gari)
1 tablespoon soy sauce

Chef's tip

Ask the fishmonger to fillet the garfish for you.

Crispy fish skin and nori Fiona Hammond

Consumers are questioning food additives, choice of organic versus GM produce and the environmental impact of food production. In the future I hope there is also a change in attitude towards using products that are often considered waste as is some offal. In the past people ate it because of necessity. We should use and creatively market these products. What does happen to all the skin from the filleted fish? This recipe uses fish skin for some tasty titbits to serve with drinks.

Method

1. Tear the nori sheet into 20 square pieces. Cut trout skin into 20 pieces. Combine salt and sansho in small bowl.
2. Press each piece of skin, flesh-side down, on to a nori square. Sprinkle the skin side generously with salt mixture.
3. Heat vegetable oil in wok until just smoking. Deep-fry a few pieces at a time for about a minute, until the skin becomes crisp and golden.
4. Remove and drain well on paper towel. Repeat with remaining skins. Serve immediately.

Ingredients Serves 4–6

2–3 sheets nori (18.5 x 20.5 cm)
4 scaled rainbow trout skins
2 teaspoons salt
1 teaspoon sansho pepper
vegetable oil, for deep-frying

Chef's tips

• Ask your fishmonger to remove the skin from 4 scaled rainbow trout fillets for you; alternatively, using a filleting knife, carefully remove the skin from each fillet yourself.
• The skinned fish fillets may be cooked as a main course or frozen for future use.
• Trevally or snapper skins work equally well.

Chorizo and beans on toast Jeremy Ryland

It is not always possible to use fresh ingredients — in practice most of us use some form of processed foods for everyday cooking. This recipe for a simple snack or light lunch uses canned beans and tomatoes, a processed chorizo sausage, pressed olive oil and the oldest processed foods of all — fresh bread and cheese.

Method

1. Heat oil in medium heavy-based saucepan; cook chorizo about 1 minute each side or until browned lightly. Remove from pan, drain on paper towel, cover to keep warm.

2. Add onion to pan, cook, stirring occasionally, 2 minutes or until onion softens. Add garlic, then tomatoes; cook gently, stirring occasionally, 2–3 minutes. Add beans and bring to a boil, stirring constantly. Reduce heat, simmer gently 5 minutes.

3. Add cooked chorizo, adjust seasonings and serve on toast, sprinkled with Parmesan cheese.

Ingredients *Serves 2*

2 tablespoons olive oil

1 chorizo, sliced diagonally into
   5 mm rounds

1 large onion (200 g), sliced thickly

2 cloves garlic, crushed

400 g can tomatoes, drained,
   chopped coarsely

430 g can three-bean mix, rinsed,
   drained

salt and black pepper, to taste

2 thick slices Italian bread,
   toasted both sides

1 tablespoon coarsely grated
   Parmesan cheese

Duck and lychee salad Barbara Lowery

Fresh lychees and barbecued duck (from a Chinese takeaway) are perfect partners for this light and easy summer salad. Ask the chef to chop the duck, then remove the flesh from the bones. Serve the salad with a glass or two of lightly chilled rosé or riesling.

Method

1. Crisp watercress in a sealed plastic bag in the refrigerator. Combine watercress, snow peas, bean sprouts and green onion in a large bowl, and toss gently.
2. Divide salad among four large serving plates and scatter with duck, lychees and almonds.
3. Drizzle dressing over salad and serve immediately.

Dressing
Whisk ingredients to combine in small bowl.

Ingredients Serves 4

1 bunch watercress (350 g), rinsed and torn into sprigs
125 g snow peas, trimmed and sliced thinly
150 g bean sprouts, trimmed
6 green onions, sliced diagonally
1 Chinese-style barbecued duck, boned and sliced
16–20 fresh lychees, peeled and seeded
$1/4$ cup (35 g) slivered almonds, toasted

Dressing
$1/4$ cup (60 ml) peanut oil
1 tablespoon cider vinegar
1 tablespoon soy sauce
2 teaspoons finely grated fresh ginger
1 teaspoon sesame oil

Seafood soufflés with Thai flavours Charmaine Solomon

Here is a cross-culture recipe marrying the flavours of the East with the techniques of the West. Needless to say, I only use my own brand of curry paste, because it has all the fresh flavours which lift Thai food into a class of its own. The quantity given is just right. If using another brand, taste as you go so that the flavour is not too hot or overwhelming. The soufflés may be made hours ahead, then refrigerated. Bring to room temperature while oven is preheating.

Method Preheat oven to moderately hot (200°C).

1. Brush eight $^3/_4$-cup (180 ml) soufflé moulds with melted butter.

2. Combine the water with salt and butter in medium heavy-based saucepan, bring to a boil. When butter melts, remove pan from heat and tip flour into pan all at once. Return to moderate heat and stir vigorously with a wooden spoon until a smooth paste forms. Remove from heat; beat in eggs, one at a time, until thoroughly mixed and paste comes away from side of pan. Leave aside.

3. Wipe fillets with damp paper towel to remove any stray scales. Cut fish into pieces and place in food processor fitted with a metal blade. Process briefly, add combined curry paste, coconut milk and salt. Process briefly to distribute flavours. Add the egg paste and process in short bursts until combined. Transfer to medium bowl.

4. Whip extra egg whites in small bowl with electric mixer until stiff; fold gently into seafood mixture. Stir in lime leaf.

5. Divide mixture among soufflé moulds, and place in a baking dish. Pour hot water around the moulds to come halfway up sides. Cook in preheated oven 20–25 minutes, or until risen and firm to the touch. Unmould onto plates; serve with a little sauce and steamed rice.

Sauce

Combine coconut milk and curry paste in small saucepan over gentle heat, add palm sugar and fish sauce to taste. Stir in lime leaf.

Chef's tip

You can use a mixture of fish and shelled, deveined uncooked prawns and/or scallops.

Ingredients Serves 8

melted butter, for brushing moulds

$^3/_4$ cup (180 ml) water

$^1/_2$ teaspoon salt

60 g butter

$^1/_3$ cup (50 g) plain flour, sifted on to baking paper square

2 eggs

400 g white fish fillets

1 $^1/_2$ tablespoons Charmaine Solomon's Thai red curry paste

$^1/_4$ cup (60 ml) coconut milk

$^1/_2$ teaspoon salt

2 egg whites, extra

1 kaffir lime leaf, shredded finely

Sauce

$^3/_4$ cup (180 ml) coconut milk

2 teaspoons Charmaine Solomon's Thai red curry paste

1 teaspoon palm sugar

1 teaspoon fish sauce

1 kaffir lime leaf, shredded finely

Duck egg pasta with kangaroo prosciutto sauce Maggie Beer

To me this represents the link between old and new Barossa and is testament to a region strong in food culture. Each ingredient has its base in the Barossa, from the local miller Laucke's flour, the duck eggs from our farm or our neighbour's, the almond flakes from Angas Park of Angaston, the olive oil and the sun-dried tomatoes. It's the smoking of the kangaroo I'm most proud of — that local ingredient married with the age-old traditions brought here by the early settlers. Although pasta is by inference Italian, the hand making of egg noodles is part of Barossa tradition.

Method

1. To make duck egg pasta: Tip flour on to bench and make a well in the centre. Whisk eggs and extra yolks together in medium bowl; pour into well. Use a fork to incorporate egg into flour until dough starts to come together, then knead dough about 10 minutes, or until shiny and firm to the touch. Form dough into a ball; flatten to a disc; wrap in plastic wrap, refrigerate 30 minutes.

2. Before beginning to roll pasta, bring a large pot of salted water to a boil. Cut refrigerated dough in half, wrap one piece carefully in plastic wrap; freeze for another use.

3. Using a pasta machine, roll the remaining dough through at fettuccine thickness several times to make it quite thin (but not to the last notch on the machine); cut into strips. Cook pasta until the water returns to a boil, strain into a colander, but do not rinse. Liberally sprinkle extra virgin olive oil over pasta. Place in serving dish, cover and leave aside.

4. To make sauce: Heat sun-dried tomatoes and almond flakes gently in olive oil, taking care not to burn or crisp the tomatoes and nuts.

5. Remove from heat and toss kangaroo prosciutto through quickly. Pile the mixture on top of hot pasta; sprinkle with Parmesan cheese.

Chef's tip

Duck eggs are perfect for this recipe as their silkiness adds to the texture, but as they are often difficult to get, you could substitute chicken eggs.

Ingredients

Duck egg pasta

500 g unbleached strong plain flour
4 x 55 g duck eggs
6 duck egg yolks, extra
extra virgin olive oil, to coat

Sauce

1/3 cup (60 g) sun-dried tomatoes, sliced thinly (avoid those packed in canola oil)
1/3 cup (25 g) toasted almond flakes
1/3 cup (60 ml) extra virgin olive oil
200 g smoked kangaroo prosciutto, sliced thinly
100 g Parmesan cheese, shaved with vegetable peeler

Tuna tartare with Melba toast Loukie Werle

Growing up in Holland, I never had a problem with eating raw ingredients, such as steak tartare and 'new' herring. When I came to Australia many years ago, it was a different story. Most people liked their steak well done and anything uncooked was treated with suspicion. So this recipe not only satisfies my own pleasure in eating good raw ingredients, it also says something about how much Australia has changed.

Method Preheat oven to moderate (180°–190°C).

1. Cut tuna into pea-sized cubes; place in medium bowl.
2. Add remaining ingredients, except lemon wedges and Melba toast, combine well with tuna. Line six $^1/_2$-cup (125 ml) ramekins or moulds with plastic wrap; divide tuna mixture evenly among moulds; press on top to pack firmly; refrigerate 1 hour.
3. Turn tartare moulds out on to plates; serve with lemon wedges and Melba toast.

Melba toast

1. Toast bread both sides. Cut off crusts and cut each slice in half horizontally. Cut each piece into two triangles and place on oven tray, cut-sides up.
2. Bake in preheated oven 10–15 minutes, or until toasts are golden and crisp. Cool on tray; store in airtight container. Makes 24.

Chef's tip

To make more substantial toasts: Remove crusts; slice bread in half diagonally, spray with olive-oil spray, bake in preheated oven for 10–15 minutes, or until toasts are golden and crisp.

Ingredients Serves 6

500 g sashimi-quality tuna
1 medium red onion (170 g), chopped finely
2 tablespoons peanut oil
1 teaspoon sesame oil
2 tablespoons sesame seeds, toasted lightly
2 teaspoons wholegrain mustard
1 red chilli, seeded, chopped finely
2 teaspoons finely chopped fresh ginger
2 teaspoons caster sugar
salt and black pepper, to taste
lemon wedges, to serve

Melba toast

6 slices thick white bread

Prawn and beetroot risotto with saffron mayonnaise Steven Snow

This recipe is a great marriage of flavours — a combination of my favourites — prawns, Pinot Noir, saffron, beetroot and green vegetables. Living and working so close to the sea, I have access to wonderful local seafood. Ask for undipped prawns for better texture and flavour.

Method

1. To make Lisbon paste: Halve capsicums; roast under grill or in very hot oven until skin blisters and blackens. Cover capsicum with plastic wrap 5 minutes; peel away skin. Remove seeds and membrane from inside capsicum.

2. Combine capsicum, garlic and salt in food processor or blender. With the motor running, add olive oil slowly to form a paste. Combine prawns and the Lisbon paste in large bowl, cover and leave aside, 10 minutes.

3. To make risotto: Combine wine, beetroot juice and stock in large saucepan, bring to a boil; reduce heat, simmer. Heat oil and butter in large frying pan over medium heat. Add onion, garlic, bay leaf and anchovy and cook until onion is golden. Add rice, stir to coat with oil. Add 1 cup (250 ml) stock mixture; cook, stirring, over low heat until liquid is absorbed. Continue adding stock in 1-cup batches, stirring, until all liquid is absorbed and rice is just tender. Adjust seasonings, stir in parsley and an extra knob of butter if desired.

4. Combine all ingredients for basting oil. Cook marinated prawns on heated oiled grill plate (or grill or barbecue) until just cooked. Brush occasionally with basting oil.

5. To serve: Place chargrilled prawns beside risotto and serve saffron mayonnaise separately. Just wilted watercress can be placed on top for added contrast and flavour.

Ingredients Serves 4

24 uncooked king prawns (approx 1.4 kg), shelled, deveined
watercress, to serve

Lisbon paste

3 medium red capsicums (600 g)
2 cloves garlic, chopped finely
$^1/_2$ teaspoon sea salt
$^1/_2$ cup (125 ml) olive oil

Risotto

1 cup (250 ml) Pinot Noir
1 cup (250 ml) beetroot juice
4 cups (1 L) chicken stock
$^1/_3$ cup (80 ml) olive oil
1 tablespoon butter
1 medium onion (150 g), sliced finely
2 cloves garlic, chopped finely
1 fresh bay leaf
4 anchovies, chopped
$1^1/_4$ cups (250 g) arborio rice
salt and black pepper, to taste
2 tablespoons finely chopped flatleaf parsley

Basting oil

100 g butter, melted

$^1/_3$ cup (80 ml) olive oil

2 cloves garlic, chopped finely

1 tablespoon finely grated
   lemon zest

1 teaspoon fresh thyme

Mayonnaise

2 egg yolks

1 cup (250 ml) vegetable oil

1 tablespoon Dijon mustard

$^1/_4$ teaspoon saffron powder

1 tablespoon white wine vinegar

salt and black pepper, to taste

Mayonnaise

1. Blend or process egg yolks; add oil gradually in a thin stream while motor is operating until mixture thickens.

2. Add mustard, saffron, vinegar, salt and pepper. Leave aside until required.

Chef's tip

Use a juice extractor to make beetroot juice. Or buy it from a fresh juice vendor.

Spaghetti with radicchio sauce Simon Johnson

This is a simple dish that goes particularly well with red wine and is good for late lunch or supper. It needs neither salt nor pepper as the capers and the radicchio provide those flavours. My mantra, as always, is that the ingredients need to be of the finest quality. As with any seasoning, use only enough freshly grated Parmesan cheese, preferably Parmigiano Reggiano, to enhance the flavour of the dish, not to overpower.

Method

1. Heat oil in large saucepan over low heat; cook onion and pancetta, stirring, 6–8 minutes, or until onion softens but is not coloured. Add garlic and cook, stirring, 2 minutes.

2. Add wine, increase heat; bring to a boil. Reduce heat, simmer uncovered until liquid reduces slightly, about 2 minutes.

3. Remove from heat; add radicchio, anchovy and capers; stir to combine.

4. Meanwhile, cook pasta in large saucepan of boiling water with sea salt, uncovered, until just tender; drain.

5. Toss pasta with sauce in large bowl. Serve immediately with Parmesan cheese.

Ingredients *Serves 4*

$1/3$ cup (80 ml) olive oil

1 large red onion (300 g), chopped finely

125 g pancetta, chopped coarsely

1 large clove garlic, sliced thinly

$1/2$ cup (125 ml) red wine

1 large trimmed tight head of raddichio (200 g), sliced finely

6 anchovy fillets, drained, chopped coarsely

2 tablespoons tiny salt-preserved capers, rinsed well

500 g durum wheat spaghetti

2 teaspoons sea salt

$1^{1}/_{4}$ cups (100 g) finely grated Parmesan cheese

Spaghetti with green tomato sauce Sue Fairlie-Cuninghame

My prediction of how I hope we will eat tomorrow is more healthily, more simply, more multiculturally; with less cooking, more focus on freshness, flavour and the quality of the ingredients, some of which may be precooked or store-bought. This dish can be served as either a starter or a main.

Method

1. Cook spaghetti in a large saucepan of salted boiling water, uncovered, until just tender; drain, reserving a little of the cooking liquid, return to pan.

2. Meanwhile, heat oil and butter in a large frying pan over low-medium heat; stir in garlic, cook 30 seconds.

3. Add tomato, cook gently 4–5 minutes, stirring occasionally. Add pesto to taste, season with sea salt and pepper.

4. Add green tomato sauce to pan with spaghetti, toss to combine, adding a little of the cooking water if it seems dry. Serve immediately on warm plates with pecorino passed separately.

Chef's tips

• Serve the green tomato sauce with pasta alternatives such as orecchiette or penne.

• Layer lasagne sheets with the green tomato sauce and top with a rich white sauce mixed with mozzarella and Parmesan cheese to taste; or serve as a sauce with gnocchi or topping for bruschetta.

• Green or unripe tomatoes add texture. They don't have a strong flavour and can also be sliced and dredged with a mix of polenta and Parmesan cheese, shallow fried in olive oil and served hot as a vegetable course.

Ingredients Serves 4

500 g spaghetti

2 teaspoons salt

$1/4$ cup (60 ml) extra virgin olive oil

1–2 tablespoons butter

1 large clove garlic, chopped finely

3 medium green tomatoes (500-600 g), diced finely

1-2 tablespoons ready-made basil pesto

sea salt and black pepper, to taste

$1^1/4$ cups (100 g) finely grated pecorino cheese

I can't believe it's not laksa Matthew Evans

This recipe first appeared in *The Sydney Morning Herald* and *The Age's* 'Good Weekend' magazine. It's yellow and coconutty, and not dissimilar to a laksa, but less complex and soupy. Fresh turmeric is fabulous, but if you can't find it, substitute turmeric powder and fry carefully with the other spices.

Method

1. Blend candlenuts with enough stock to make a paste. Reserve.

2. Heat oil in medium saucepan; cook onion, stirring occasionally, until soft. Add turmeric; cook gently 1 minute. Stir in chilli and spices and cook 30 seconds. Add nut paste and remaining stock; bring to a boil. Add coconut cream, reduce heat to a simmer; add fish sauce and lime juice.

3. Stir in chicken; reheat, adjust seasonings, adding more fish sauce (instead of salt), chilli and lime juice if desired.

4. Meanwhile, rinse noodles under hot water; drain. Transfer to large bowl, separate noodles with fork.

5. Divide noodles between bowls, ladle chicken and sauce over; serve topped with bean sprouts and coriander.

Ingredients *Serves 2*

5 candlenuts (or substitute macadamia kernels if absolutely necessary)

$2^{1}/_{2}$ cups (625 ml) chicken stock

2 teaspoons oil

$^{1}/_{2}$ small onion (40 g), chopped finely

5 g fresh turmeric, peeled, grated finely or 1 teaspoon of turmeric powder

$^{1}/_{4}$ teaspoon chilli powder, or to taste

$^{1}/_{2}$ teaspoon ground coriander seeds

$^{1}/_{4}$ teaspoon ground cumin

$^{1}/_{2}$ cup (125 ml) coconut cream

3 teaspoons fish sauce

juice of $^{1}/_{2}$ lime, strained (approx 1 tablespoon)

200 g cooked chicken in bite-sized shreds

400 g fresh rice noodles

40 g bean sprouts, soaked in cold water 10 minutes, drained

2 tablespoons coriander leaves, chopped finely

Barramundi in banana leaves with curried chickpeas Luke Mangan

Barramundi is one of my favourite fish — I find its earthy flavours easy to work with. This dish is pretty simple, you can change the spices around if you like and add some fresh herbs. You don't have to wrap it in banana leaves — you could bake it in foil if you like. If you can't buy barra use any other fish you can get.

Method *Preheat oven to moderately hot (200°–210°C).*

1. Crush cumin, coriander and mustard seeds coarsely in mortar and pestle, or small bowl of food processor.
2. Place spice mixture in a small bowl, add olive oil; mix to a coarse paste. Rub paste all over fish.
3. Place fish on one end of banana leaf and roll up tightly, leaving head and tail exposed. Repeat with remaining fish and banana leaves.
4. Place fish parcels in large, lined baking dish, seam-side down. Bake, uncovered, in preheated oven 15–20 minutes, or until fish is cooked through when tested with a knife.
5. Serve fish on fresh banana leaves, with curried chickpeas and steamed bok choy.

Curried chickpeas

1. Heat oil in medium frying pan; cook onion, stirring, 2 minutes or until soft. Add curry powder, cook, stirring, 1 minute, or until fragrant.
2. Add chickpeas and coconut milk, stir to combine; bring to a boil. Reduce heat, simmer, uncovered, 5 minutes.
3. Blend or process one third of chickpea mixture until smooth; return to pan with remaining whole chickpea mixture. Mix well, season; leave aside, covered to keep warm until ready to serve.

Ingredients *Serves 4*

$1/4$ cup cumin seeds
$1/4$ cup coriander seeds
$1 1/2$ tablespoons yellow mustard seeds
$1/3$ cup (80 ml) extra virgin olive oil
4 plate-sized whole barramundi, cleaned
4 x 40 cm lengths banana leaf
500 g baby bok choy, trimmed, halved

Curried chickpeas

1 tablespoon extra virgin olive oil
1 onion, chopped finely
2 teaspoons curry powder
2 x 300 g cans chickpeas, drained
400 ml can (approx $1 2/3$ cups) coconut milk
sea salt and black pepper, to taste

Duck with star anise and date purée Di Holuigue

Here is one of our favourite restaurant meats made into a roast for the home kitchen with a sauce that can be made well in advance. The not-so-classic sauce is a fusion of the traditional French base for sauces — the demi-glace — with the addition of cinnamon and star anise, spices usually used by the French only in desserts, but close to the Australian heart because of our familiarity with Asian flavourings.

Method *Preheat oven to hot (225°C).*

1. Cut off duck wings at the second joint (the joint nearest the duck). Remove neck. Keep these for the demi-glace, along with the heart and gizzard. Truss the duck.

2. Place duck in a greased baking dish, smear with butter, sprinkle with salt and pepper. Roast in preheated oven 15 minutes; reduce temperature to moderate (180°C), roast 1³/₄ hours. Remove from oven and cover to keep warm.

3. To make sauce: Combine demi-glace in a medium saucepan with red wine, orange juice, star anise, cinnamon, bay leaf, shallot and black peppercorns. Bring to a boil; reduce heat, simmer until sauce reduces by at least a third. Strain into heatproof jug. Pour off grease from baking dish; add a little water to boil and scrape the sediments. Strain into the jug, stir to combine with demi-glace mixture; season with salt and pepper. A touch of brandy or sherry can be added if needed to cut the sweetness.

4. To serve: Cut duck into four portions. Cut from the parson's nose along each side of the backbone; discard backbone. Cut each half into wing and leg sections. Serve on a pool of sauce with a spoonful of date purée alongside and a potato accompaniment of your choice. Serve remaining sauce separately.

Demi-glace

1. Melt margarine in large stockpot over high heat; fry beef and duck trimmings as brown as possible. Add carrot and onion and continue browning. Even the carrot edges must be coloured before proceeding. The colour obtained at this point is crucial to the success of the sauce.

2. Add flour, stir to a paste. Add stock, wine, the water, remaining vegetables, bouquet garni, clove, beef cube (to reinforce the flavour, not as a substitute for stock), tomato paste and salt and pepper.

3. Bring to a boil, reduce heat and simmer, uncovered, for a minimum of 2 hours, preferably 4–5 hours. During this time, evaporation will take place and the loss can be replaced by water. This is beneficial,

Ingredients *Serves 4*

1 x 2–2.4 kg duckling
60 g butter
salt and black pepper, to taste

Sauce

2 cups (500 ml) demi-glace
¹/₂ cup (125 ml) red wine
¹/₂ cup (125 ml) orange juice
¹/₂ star anise
small piece cinnamon stick
1 small bay leaf
1 tablespoon chopped shallot
2 black peppercorns
salt and black pepper, to taste
brandy or sherry, to taste

Demi-glace

75 g margarine
150 g beef trimmings, including muscle but no fat
duck neck, heart, wingtips and gizzard
2 medium carrots (240 g), sliced thinly
2 medium onions (300 g), chopped finely
1 tablespoon plain flour
4 cups (1L) beef stock
1 cup (250 ml) dry white wine
1 cup (250 ml) water
4 shallots, chopped finely
2 cloves garlic, crushed

¼ turnip (60 g), chopped finely

½ medium leek (175 g), sliced
   thinly

1 trimmed stick celery (75 g),
   sliced thinly

mushroom parings, a little onion
   skin to intensify the colour,
   optional

large bouquet garni (parsley,
   thyme — no bay leaf)

1 clove

1 beef cube

2 teaspoons tomato paste

salt and black pepper, to taste

Date purée

15 fresh dates, seeded

pinch bicarbonate of soda

1 tablespoon butter

salt and black pepper, to taste

pinch ground cumin

¼ cup (60 ml) cream

because the evaporation will have caused solids to caramelise on the edge of the pot. Brushing this down constantly and stirring it through the liquid increases both the colour and the strength of flavour. Strain demi-glace through a metal sieve, forcing with a whisk to extract as much liquid as possible.

Date purée

1. Combine dates with bicarbonate of soda and butter in a medium saucepan. Just cover with water, bring to a boil; reduce heat, simmer until tender.

2. Purée, preferably through a mouli for the smoothest texture, or in a blender or food processor. Season with salt, pepper and cumin; stir in cream.

Chef's tips

• Beef trimmings can be the parings of a beef fillet, 3 or 4 cubes of gravy beef, or minced topside.

• Use margarine instead of butter when preparing demi-glace, as butter burns before the necessary level of browning is achieved.

• The demi-glace can be used immediately, stored up to 5 days in the refrigerator, or frozen in small lidded containers indefinitely. This re-inforced beef stock gives better body to sauces than reduced stock.

Roasted rack of lamb with miso Tetsuya Wakuda

Lamb is something many people are reluctant to cook, as they don't like the smell. Cooking it this way, the miso rounds out the aroma, making it more appetising. The blue cheese is a very subtle means of enhancing the flavours of this global village inspired combination. If you prefer a more defined blue cheese flavour, double the quantity.

Method *Preheat oven to very slow (120°C).*

1. Place witlof in small baking dish and pour over 1 cup (250 ml) chicken stock. Add 2 tablespoons of the grapeseed oil; season with sugar, sea salt and white pepper. Cover with aluminium foil; bake in preheated oven 1 hour, or until witlof is tender. Leave aside, covered.

2. Season lamb racks with salt and pepper.

3. Heat the remaining grapeseed oil in large frying pan until it smokes. Seal the lamb quickly until browned lightly.

4. Line baking dish with thyme and place lamb racks on top. Place in the oven and roast 45 minutes, or until cooked as desired. Remove from oven and leave aside, covered, to keep warm.

5. Meanwhile, to make sauce: Bring the chicken stock to a boil in small saucepan. Add miso paste and simmer, stirring, until paste dissolves. Add cheese and cook, stirring, until cheese melts and sauce thickens slightly. Add soy sauce, mirin and ginger, stirring constantly. Remove from heat and strain sauce through a sieve. Adjust seasonings.

6. Slice lamb from each rack in one piece by carving lengthways along the bone. Discard bones and cut lamb into thick rounds.

7. Blanch snow pea sprouts in boiling water, drain. Arrange sprouts on serving plates. Top with witlof and lamb. Spoon over miso sauce. Garnish with green onion and chives; sprinkle with sesame seeds.

Ingredients *Serves 4–6*

2 medium witlof (250 g), quartered lengthways
1 cup (250 ml) chicken stock
5 tablespoons (100 ml) grapeseed oil
pinch caster sugar
sea salt and white pepper, to taste
4 small racks of lamb with 6 cutlets per rack, trimmed
1 bunch thyme
150 g snow pea sprouts
1 green onion, sliced thinly
1 tablespoon finely chopped chives
1 teaspoon black sesame seeds

Sauce

1 cup (250 ml) chicken stock
$1/4$ cup (100 g) white miso paste
20 g blue cheese
1 teaspoon soy sauce
1 teaspoon mirin (sweet rice wine)
1 teaspoon finely grated fresh ginger
salt and pepper, to taste

Quail in pandanus leaves Jacques Reymond

I created this recipe as I was walking through the bush at Turtle Island in Fiji. I smelt some beautiful leaves — they were pandanus. They had a partly smoky aroma, and this gave me an idea to create a dish that would retain these fragrant flavours.

Method *Preheat oven to slow (150ºC).*

1. To make glaze: Bring honey and spices to a boil in a small saucepan; reduce heat, simmer until mixture reduces to a heavy syrup. Add vinegar and soy sauce; simmer until glaze reduces to a syrupy consistency. Leave aside.

2. To make farce: Melt ghee in baking dish, arrange quail in dish, brush with some of the glaze, coat with ghee, sprinkle with salt and pepper; bake in preheated oven 8–10 minutes, or until quail are just cooked and still pink in the middle. Remove from dish, cut quail into cubes. Combine shallot, garlic, ginger and chilli in baking dish and stir over low heat until shallot wilts. Combine shallot mixture with diced quail, soy sauce, hoisin sauce and coriander in medium bowl.

3. Lay quail skin-side down on chopping board, spoon farce inside and shape into a neat ball. Cut each pandanus leaf lengthways into four strips and weave strips into a small open lattice. Repeat with remaining strips to make four woven mats. Place a quail on top of each mat and wrap it up. Trim leaves evenly with scissors, secure ends of parcels with aluminium foil.

4. Increase oven temperature to hot (220ºC). Brush quail through leaves with glaze, place on baking dish lined with non-stick baking paper; bake in preheated oven 10–12 minutes, brushing with glaze halfway through cooking time.

5. Steam bok choy until just tender, stir-fry in wok with shallot, ginger and smoked eel. Divide bok choy mixture among serving plates. Top with quail; spoon dressing over.

Ingredients *Serves 4*

Glaze

$1/3$ cup (120 g) honey
1 teaspoon cardamom seeds
$1/2$ teaspoon Sichuan pepper
1 teaspoon cracked black pepper
$1/8$ teaspoon finely chopped
   juniper berries
$1^{1}/_{2}$ tablespoons malt vinegar
3 teaspoons soy sauce

Farce

1 tablespoon ghee
   (clarified butter)
2 quail, boned
salt and black pepper, to taste
2 shallots, sliced thinly
1 clove garlic, sliced thinly
1 teaspoon julienned fresh ginger,
   blanched twice
$1/2$ teaspoon finely chopped chilli
1 teaspoon soy sauce
$1/2$ teaspoon hoisin sauce
1 teaspoon coriander leaves

4 quail, boned

4 pandanus leaves

8 baby bok choy

1 shallot, sliced thinly

1 teaspoon julienned fresh ginger,
   blanched twice

70 g smoked eel, cut into
   small cubes

Dressing

bones of 6 quail

4 cups (1 L) water

1 tablespoon mirin

1 tablespoon hazelnut oil

2 teaspoons walnut oil

1 teaspoon salt-reduced soy
   sauce

2 teaspoons balsamic vinegar

2 teaspoons finely chopped garlic

2 teaspoons finely chopped
   blanched fresh ginger

2 teaspoons roasted yellow
   mustard seeds

2 teaspoons roasted cardamom
   seeds

$1/4$ cup (60 ml) hot reduced
   quail stock

Dressing

Combine quail bones with the water in medium saucepan. Bring to a boil; reduce heat, simmer gently until stock reduces to about $1/4$ cup of liquid. Strain stock into small heatproof jug, discard bones. Whisk remaining ingredients together in small bowl to form an emulsion. Stir in hot reduced quail stock.

Chef's tip

To clarify butter, melt butter in small saucepan without browning, remove from heat; stand until milky solids settle to the base of pan. Pour off clear yellow liquid and allow to solidify. Discard residue, or use to enrich sauces or soups.

Pork with Chinese flavours Lyndey Milan

The future heralds a return to flavour, rejecting diets, fads and artificially created food, and, learning from our multicultural society, valuing taking time to eat, and doing so without guilt. While still streamlining techniques, we will be prepared to spend more than 10 minutes in the kitchen for the benefits that flow from home cooking. I also believe in reconciliation through food. If you enjoy food from another culture, surely you must appreciate the other values of that culture?

Method

1. Bring a large saucepan of water to a boil and cook pork belly 2 minutes. Drain, refresh pork in cold water. Repeat twice so that pork is blanched and refreshed three times altogether. Score rind of pork.

2. Combine remaining ingredients in large saucepan; bring to a boil. Add pork, skin-side up, return to a boil; simmer 1 hour. Ensure liquid comes just up to pork skin; add more water if it is much below it.

3. Remove pork from saucepan, place on tray under preheated grill. Grill until crisp, about 8–10 minutes. Strain cooking liquid into medium jug; discard solids.

4. Meanwhile, heat oils in wok and stir-fry garlic, chilli and ginger until fragrant. Add mushroom, gai laan and green onion; stir-fry until just wilted. Moisten with some of the strained cooking liquid.

5. Rinse noodles under hot water; drain. Transfer to large bowl, separate noodles with fork.

6. Slice pork thinly and serve on top of noodles and vegetables. Spoon a little more reserved cooking liquid over the top.

Chef's tips

• Master stock spices are also known as Chinese mixed spices and comprise ingredients including fennel, anise, ginger, chilli, orange peel, cassia bark, liquorice root and cloves. Master stock spices can be mail ordered from Herbie's, Ph: (02) 9555-6035, email: herbie@herbies.com.au.

• After use, strain cooking liquid, refrigerate; remove any fat that rises to the top and freeze for later use.

Ingredients Serves 4

800 g whole piece belly pork
30 g master stock spices
1/2 cup (125 ml) soy sauce
4 cups (1 L) water
1/4 cup (60 ml) Chinese black
   vinegar
1/4 cup (60 ml) dry sherry

To serve

1 teaspoon sesame oil
1 tablespoon olive oil
2 cloves garlic, crushed
2 red chillies, seeded and
   sliced thinly
2 teaspoons finely chopped
   fresh ginger
8 shiitake mushrooms, stems
   sliced thinly, caps sliced thickly
500 g gai laan (Chinese broccoli),
   leaves separated
4 green onions, sliced thinly
500 g fresh rice noodles

Bernard's best pumped rack of lamb Bernard King

This is the only recipe that Margaret Fulton has ever requested from me! The style began with a pumped leg of lamb. I was planning to stage a large glamorous party for visiting Olympic VIPs and I decided that rack should perform as well as leg — so I experimented with resounding success! You may need to give your butcher notice to pump the racks for you. Precise measurements are not my thing, but your editor strong-armed me into providing them. Feel free to adjust the amounts to make your own sensational version.

Editor's note: Sadly, Bernard King passed away just as we were going to press. A true pro to the end, Bernard managed, although protesting with his trademark wit and charm, to comply with our request for quantities. He will be sadly missed by the food media. Vale Bernard.

Method *Preheat oven to moderate (180°C).*

1. Combine lamb racks with honey, bay leaves and allspice and water to cover in large stockpot, bring to a boil. Reduce heat to a very slow simmer, cook, covered, 40 minutes or until meat is fork tender; cool in cooking liquid, drain. Trim fat and bones.
2. To make glaze: Heat oil in medium frying pan, add ginger, mustard seeds and quince jelly; cook, stirring, until jelly melts.
3. Arrange lamb racks in large baking dish, brush with glaze and bake in preheated oven 30 minutes. To serve, carve individual cutlets at the table. Stand for the applause!

Ingredients *Serves 10*

5 pumped racks of lamb
$1/4$ cup (90 g) dark honey
3 bay leaves
1 tablespoon ground allspice

Glaze

1 tablespoon oil
1 cup slivered fresh ginger
2 tablespoons white mustard
  seeds
375 g quince jelly

Beef with caramelised onions and mustard sauce Jenny Sheard

I suspect the food of tomorrow will be going retro, with a return to flavour, goodness and a producer's guarantee a product has not been messed with. There will come a time when a product can be bought with an identifying label, outlining growing conditions, or the foodstuffs that have been fed to the bird or animal throughout its life.

Method

1. To caramelise onion: Melt 1 tablespoon of the oil with butter in medium heavy-based frying pan on medium-to-low heat. Add onion, cook, covered, stirring frequently, 15 minutes. Reduce heat if onion begins to burn. Uncover pan, increase heat slightly; add salt and sugar. Cook, stirring frequently, 10 minutes; transfer onion to heatproof bowl, leave aside, covered, to keep warm.

2. Using same frying pan, heat remaining oil over medium-to-high heat; cook steaks 3 minutes each side or until cooked as desired. Transfer steaks to a plate, cover to keep warm; rest 10 minutes. Reserve juices.

3. Add beef stock to pan, reduce by half over high heat. Add mustard, crème fraiche or sour cream and reserved beef juices. Whisk sauce about 1 minute to incorporate all ingredients.

4. To serve: Divide caramelised onion among four plates. Place each fillet on top and drizzle with sauce. Lightly steamed broccolini dressed with lemon juice and extra virgin olive oil is an excellent accompaniment.

Ingredients Serves 4

2 tablespoons extra virgin olive oil

25 g butter

3 medium onions (450 g), sliced finely

1 teaspoon salt

$1/2$ teaspoon sugar

4 x 180 g beef eye fillet steaks

$1 1/4$ cups (310 ml) beef stock

2 teaspoons Dijon mustard

2 teaspoons crème fraiche or sour cream

Roast chicken crusted with Australian spices Ian Hemphill

Although many spices now produced in Australia had their origins elsewhere, like Australians themselves, they have the potential to function in harmony with those that are indigenous to Australia. This recipe uses flavours native to this land, in conjunction with locally grown, non-indigenous spices. Serve with steamed Warrigul greens (a native spinach), or another green vegetable of choice.

Method *Preheat oven to moderate (180°–190°C).*

1. Combine spices and salt in small bowl.

2. Coat chicken with spice mixture; refrigerate, covered, at least 1 hour.

3. Coat baking dish lightly with olive oil spray, place chicken in oiled dish and spray chicken lightly with olive oil. Roast, uncovered, in pre-heated oven 45 minutes.

4. Meanwhile, cook potato in boiling water until just tender; drain. Remove baking dish from oven, place potatoes around chicken. Return to oven, roast, uncovered, 20 minutes. Turn potatoes once or twice during cooking time. Chicken is cooked when a skewer inserted into the thigh releases clear juices. Place chicken and potatoes on platter; cover to keep warm.

5. Drain pan juices into cup leaving 2 tablespoons pan juices in dish. Place dish on low heat, stir flour in gradually. Remove excess oil from reserved pan juices with a spoon, stir pan juice into flour mixture; cook 1 minute, or until sauce is thick and smooth.

6. Carve chicken and serve with potatoes, sauce and zucchini flowers.

Chef's tip

Spices can be mail ordered from Herbie's, Ph: (02) 9555-6035, email: herbie@herbies.com.au

Ingredients *Serves 4*

3 teaspoons ground coriander seeds

1 teaspoon ground bush tomato (akudjura)

$1/2$ teaspoon ground lemon myrtle leaf

$1/2$ teaspoon roasted ground wattleseed

$1/2$ teaspoon ground ginger

$1/4$ teaspoon ground native pepperberry

$1/4$ teaspoon salt

1.2–1.4 kg chicken

olive-oil spray

12 (500 g) kipfler potatoes, chopped coarsely

2 teaspoons plain flour

steamed zucchini flowers, to serve

Sugar 'n spice oxtail Kate McGhie

Coming from a beef breeding background, I see how this recipe reflects the dynamic changes in Australian food. In just one generation, from overcooked pan-fried beef steak to an unctuous cheaper cut beef dish inspired by the meld of cultures, it represents our new-found culinary confidence.

Method *Preheat oven to moderately slow (170°C).*

1. Heat oil in large non-stick frying pan; cook oxtail, turning occasionally, until well browned. Transfer oxtail to large baking dish.

2. Combine palm sugar, ginger, garlic, star anise, cinnamon, chilli sauce, kecap manis, stock and citrus zests in small bowl. Pour mixture over meat, cover with aluminium foil; cook in preheated oven, about $2\frac{1}{2}$ hours, or until meat is falling from bones and sticky.

3. Remove from oven and allow oxtail to cool in own juices.

4. To make toffee nuts: Heat chilli oil and palm sugar in a small frying pan; add peanuts. Toss and cook until nuts caramelise. Spoon peanuts on to plate lined with non-stick baking paper to cool.

5. To make salad: Combine all ingredients on serving platter.

6. To serve: Remove meat from bones while still warm and arrange on salad. Garnish with toffee nuts.

Ingredients *Serves 6*

1 tablespoon vegetable oil
2 oxtails, jointed, or 8 large thick pieces of oxtail
$\frac{2}{3}$ cup (180 g) shaved palm sugar
1 tablespoon finely grated fresh ginger
2 cloves garlic, crushed
3 teaspoons ground star anise
1 stick cinnamon
$\frac{1}{3}$ cup (80 ml) sweet chilli sauce
$\frac{1}{3}$ cup (80 ml) kecap manis
1 cup (250 ml) chicken stock
2 strips lemon zest
2 strips orange zest

Toffee nuts

1 tablespoon chilli oil
2 tablespoons shaved palm sugar
$\frac{3}{4}$ cup (110 g) coarsely chopped peanuts

Salad

3 cups finely shredded cabbage
$\frac{1}{2}$ cup (125 ml) rice wine
1 tablespoon toasted sesame seeds
$\frac{1}{3}$ cup deep-fried shallots
$\frac{1}{2}$ cup coriander leaves
1 cup (80 g) bean sprouts

Crushed raspberry semifreddo Donna Hay

Semifreddo is Italian for half frozen — it's like ice-cream but you don't need the same kind of fancy gadgets to make it at home. It's the perfect dessert for the laid-back spirit of summer when everyone is relaxed, restraint goes out the window, we happily accept second helpings as big as the first and say yes to any sweet treat any time of the day or night. The beauty of semifreddo, apart from it's ease of preparation, is that it has to be made in advance, stored in the freezer and scooped into cones or sliced whenever the fancy strikes.

Method

1. Beat cream in medium bowl with electric mixer until very soft peaks form. (Any stiffer and it will be difficult to incorporate into semifreddo.) Cover and refrigerate until required.
2. Place eggs, extra yolks, vanilla and sugar in medium heatproof bowl; stand bowl over saucepan of simmering water (don't let the base of the bowl touch the water), whisk mixture 4–5 minutes, or until heated through, sugar dissolves and mixture is frothy.
3. Remove bowl from heat and beat with electric mixer 3–5 minutes, or until pale and thick.
4. Crush 300g of the raspberries lightly and fold gently through the egg mixture. Fold in whipped cream until just combined.
5. Line base and sides of an 8 x 26-cm loaf pan with non-stick baking paper. Arrange remaining raspberries in bottom of pan and pour semifreddo mixture on top. Cover with aluminium foil; freeze 4–6 hours or until firm.
6. To serve, remove semifreddo from pan and cut into thick slices.

Chef's tips

• The recipe can be made ahead, but if left any longer than three days in the freezer the mixture will not be as light and fluffy.
• If the semifreddo is too firm, leave at room temperature for 5–10 minutes before serving.

Ingredients Serves 8

1^3/$_4$ cups (430 ml) cream
3 eggs
2 egg yolks, extra
^{1}/$_2$ teaspoon vanilla extract
1 cup (220 g) caster sugar
500 g raspberries, fresh or frozen

Hot pavlovas with Frangelico sauce and praline Pamela Clark

These meringues aren't far from being a flourless soufflé really, and they'll deflate as they cool, so it's important to transfer them quickly, with an egg slide, from the oven tray to the serving plates. The boiling water meringue recipe is nothing new but icing sugar mixture (the cornflour in the icing sugar mixture adds stability to the meringue) replaces white sugar. Both the sauce and praline could be made ahead.

Method Preheat oven to moderate (160°C fan-forced).

1. Place oven shelves as low as possible in oven. Grease and line two oven trays with non-stick baking paper; trace three 10-cm circles about 6 cm apart on each tray.
2. Beat egg whites, icing sugar mixture and the boiling water in small bowl with electric mixer, about 8 minutes or until soft peaks form. Ladle egg white mixture equally among the six circles.
3. Bake on lowest shelves of preheated oven about 20 minutes or until meringue feels set.
4. Meanwhile, beat cream in small bowl until soft peaks form.
5. Top hot pavlovas with cream, drizzle with warm Frangelico sauce and sprinkle with crushed hazelnut praline. Decorate with praline shards; serve immediately.

Chocolate Frangelico sauce

Stir chocolate, cream and Frangelico in small saucepan over low heat until chocolate melts; keep warm.

Hazelnut praline

1. Place hazelnuts in single layer on greased oven tray. Combine sugar and the water in small saucepan; stir over heat, without boiling, until sugar dissolves. Bring to a boil; reduce heat, simmer, uncovered, without stirring, until mixture turns golden brown.
2. Pour sugar mixture evenly over hazelnuts; cool. Break praline into shards; process one-third of the shards until crushed.

Ingredients Serves 6

3 egg whites
2 cups (320 g) icing sugar mixture
$1/2$ cup (125 ml) boiling water
300 ml thickened cream

Chocolate Frangelico sauce

150 g dark chocolate, chopped
    coarsely
$3/4$ cup (180 ml) thickened cream
2 tablespoons Frangelico

Hazelnut praline

$2/3$ cup (100 g) roasted hazelnuts,
    chopped coarsely
1 cup (220 g) caster sugar
$1/2$ cup (125 ml) water

Goat's milk panna cotta with Champagne jelly Steve Manfredi

This panna cotta is a perfect example of the flavour of Italy from the produce of Australia. Use good Champagne for the jelly and buy dried mango from a health food shop. Mango offers many sculptural possibilities, so you can experiment with the way you cut it for different decorative effects.

Method

1. Place milk in medium saucepan over low heat and bring slowly to simmering point. Do not allow to boil.

2. Whisk yolks and sugar in a medium bowl 3 minutes, or until mixture is pale in colour. Add hot milk slowly and whisk to combine. Pour egg mixture into cleaned saucepan; cook, stirring 10–15 minutes, or until custard coats the back of the spoon. Pour custard into cleaned bowl.

3. Squeeze out excess water from gelatine leaves; add to warm custard, stir until gelatine dissolves. Refrigerate until cool.

4. Once slight setting occurs, stir in whipped cream. Grease six $3/4$-cup (180 ml) moulds or ramekins. Divide custard mixture among moulds, tap bases on bench to remove any air bubbles; refrigerate, covered, about 4 hours or until set.

5. Dip moulds in bowl of boiling water for 30 seconds, turn panna cottas on to serving plates; serve with fresh and dried mango and Champagne jelly.

Champagne jelly

1. Bring Champagne to a boil in medium saucepan, add sugar; stir until sugar dissolves. Squeeze out excess water from gelatine leaves; add to hot liquid, stir until gelatine dissolves.

2. Pour gelatine mixture into flat container and refrigerate 2 hours, or until set. Crush jelly roughly with a fork before serving.

Ingredients Serves 6

2 cups (500 ml) goat's milk
6 egg yolks
$1/3$ cup (75 g) sugar
3 x 5 g gelatine leaves, soaked in cold water
1 cup (250 ml) thickened cream, whipped
1 large mango (600 g), sliced thinly
2 slices dried mango, shredded finely

Champagne jelly

500 ml (2 cups) Champagne
$1/2$ cup (110 g) caster sugar
3 x 5 g gelatine leaves, soaked in cold water

Liqueur fruit ice-creams with macerated cherries Jan Purser

Being a nutrition consultant, I am often asked for delicious, healthy recipes. This recipe fits the criteria, being perfect for a Christmas dessert or a special and easy dessert all year round. As a bonus, it's also relatively low in fat. You can make the ice-cream up to four days ahead and the macerated cherries up to a day ahead.

Method

1. Combine figs, apricots, sultanas and currants in medium glass or ceramic bowl. Stir in Cointreau, cover; leave aside overnight to macerate, stirring occasionally.
2. Line bases of eight ¹/₂-cup (125 ml) timbale moulds with non-stick baking paper. Place moulds on freezer tray.
3. Place ice-cream in large mixing bowl and refrigerate for 15–20 minutes to soften slightly. Add dried fruit mixture and mixed spice to ice-cream; use a wooden spoon to combine.
4. Spoon ice-cream mixture into prepared timbale moulds, pressing in firmly. Cover with plastic wrap; freeze overnight.
5. Place chocolate in small heatproof bowl over a small saucepan of simmering water. Stir with a dry metal spoon until melted and smooth.
6. To serve: Remove ice-cream from moulds by running a knife around edges; turn out on to serving plates, remove and discard baking paper. Drizzle with chocolate and serve with macerated cherries.

Macerated cherries

Combine cherries, sugar and Cointreau in medium non-reactive bowl. Cover; refrigerate at least 4 hours.

Chef's tip

If you can't buy fresh cherries, use a 300 g packet frozen cherries, thawed following directions on the packet.

Ingredients Makes 8

- ³/₄ cup (140 g) finely chopped dried figs
- ¹/₂ cup (75 g) finely chopped moist dried apricots
- ²/₃ cup (110 g) sultanas
- ²/₃ cup (100 g) currants
- ¹/₃ cup (80 ml) Cointreau
- 1 L vanilla reduced-fat ice-cream
- 1 teaspoon mixed spice
- 50 g dark chocolate, chopped coarsely

Macerated cherries

- 300 g cherries, pitted, quartered
- 1 tablespoon caster sugar
- 1¹/₂ tablespoons Cointreau

Chocolate chilli truffles Victor Pisapia

Ancient Aztecs first combined chocolate and chilli for royalty and warriors to drink. Chilli develops the bitter-sweet characters of chocolate and adds a warming tingle. Just as Australia marches to its own drummer, this recipe moves the past into the future — an ancient combination that is still innovative.

Method

1. Combine chocolate, butter and cream in the top of a double boiler over pan of simmering water, stir until melted. Whisk in chilli powder; mix until smooth.

2. Remove saucepan from heat. Pour chocolate mixture into shallow baking dish; cover, refrigerate at least 4 hours.

3. Score the top of the firm mixture into equally sized portions for the number of truffles you want to make. Line an oven tray with non-stick baking paper.

4. Scoop up the truffle mixture with a spoon or ice-cream scoop. Roll the truffles into balls between your palms.

5. Melt extra chocolate in top of double boiler over simmering water, dip truffles in chocolate until coated all over. Place finished truffles on to prepared oven tray; refrigerate at least 1 hour.

Chef's tip

Don't buy commercial chilli powders that often contain salt and other undesirable ingredients. I recommend using a pure powdered cayenne chilli.

Ingredients *Makes about 14*

340 g couverture chocolate
15 g unsalted butter
1 cup (250 ml) cream
$1/2$ teaspoon chilli powder
280 g couverture chocolate, extra, for dipping

Macadamia coconut syrup cake Sheridan Rogers

This delightful cake makes a wonderful gift, especially when wrapped in cellophane and tied with a bow. The combination of macadamia nuts and lemon myrtle makes for a unique Aussie flavour and the inclusion of shredded coconut lends a lovely texture.

Method *Preheat oven to moderate (180º–190ºC fan-forced).*

1. Grease and line a 22-cm-round springform cake pan. Blend or process macadamia nuts until coarsely chopped (take care not to process to a paste). Combine chopped nuts in a large bowl with flour and coconut.

2. Beat egg yolks with $1/3$ cup (75 g) of the sugar and vanilla in small bowl with electric mixer 3 minutes, or until pale and creamy. Fold in half the macadamia and flour mixture, then melted butter, then the remaining macadamia mixture.

3. Beat egg whites in small bowl with electric mixer until soft peaks form; gradually add remaining sugar and beat until firm and glossy. Fold whites gently through cake mixture, a third at a time. Spoon mixture into prepared pan.

4. Bake in preheated oven 50 minutes, or until a skewer tests clean (you may need to cover with aluminium foil if browning too quickly).

5. Remove from oven, brush with syrup; stand in pan 10 minutes. Turn cake out; decorate with shredded coconut and native berries.

Syrup

1. Bring sugar and the water to a boil in small saucepan. Reduce heat, simmer gently until sugar dissolves. Remove from heat.

2. When bubbles stop, stir in lemon myrtle; leave aside to infuse 10 minutes. Strain syrup through fine sieve.

Chef's tip

We used whole quandong, small wild limes and riberries to decorate the cake. These native fruit can be bought from The Essential Ingredient, Ph: (02) 9550 5477.

Ingredients *Serves 8*

1 cup (150 g) raw unsalted macadamias

$1/3$ cup (50 g) self-raising flour, sifted

$1/2$ cup (35 g) shredded coconut

3 eggs, separated

$2/3$ cup (150 g) caster sugar

1 teaspoon vanilla essence

100 g unsalted butter, melted and cooled

shredded coconut and native berries for decoration

Syrup

$1/3$ cup (75 g) caster sugar

$1/3$ cup (80 ml) water

3 teaspoons ground lemon myrtle

Biographies

Stephanie Alexander, chef and food writer, is currently the creative partner behind the busy Richmond Hill Cafe & Larder in Melbourne. She is the author of 10 books including *The Cook's Companion* and *Cooking & Travelling in South-West France*. In mid-2001, she initiated an innovative primary school program involving gardening, cooking and food appreciation called The Kitchen Garden at Collingwood College. For more information see www.stephaniealexander.com.au.

Mary Atkins, former President of the Food Media Club, is a food economist and managing director of a niche marketing company providing support to the food and wine industry. During 18 years of business, her company has supplied test kitchen facilities, cooking classes and mobile consumer advisory kitchens for food retailers. The company now specialises in marketing and event management.

Maggie Beer settled in South Australia's Barossa Valley in 1973 with her husband Colin, where they established the Pheasant Farm Restaurant. Maggie's career now spans farming, export, food production and writing. Her books are *Maggie's Farm, Maggie's Orchard, Maggie's Table, Cooking with Verjuice* and *Stephanie and Maggie's Tuscan Cookbook* (with Stephanie Alexander). In 2001 Maggie won the Food Media Club Industry Peer Award for Best Overall Contribution to Print Medium. For more information see www.maggiebeer.com.au.

Sue Bennett is editor of *The Daily Telegraph's* weekly liftout, Food & Wine. A journalist almost all her working life, she has undertaken most newspaper roles including editor of a regional newspaper. English born and daughter of a wonderful home cook, she spent much of her childhood in France, from which she traces her interest in food and wine.

Janelle Bloom is the author of three cookbooks. Considered Australia's leading microwave cook, she has been writing and teaching microwave and traditional cooking for more than 15 years. A regular presenter with Channel 9 for seven years, she also contributes regularly to many of Australia's leading food publications.

Jan Boon was instrumental in the relaunch of the Australian Gas Cooking School, with the introduction of specialty chef's classes and gourmet tours. For the past 40 years she has been involved in teaching, writing, radio and television, developing competitions and judging at regional and major shows, such as the Royal Easter Show.

Jo Anne Calabria, a former President of the Food Media Club, has more than 20 years experience as a food industry professional. She is a food editor and stylist, cookbook author and food broadcaster. Prior to her commencing her own food consultancy in 2001, Jo Anne was Food Editor at *Family Circle* for more than a decade.

Joan Campbell started her cooking career catering, giving cooking classes and writing restaurant reviews for *The Sunday Telegraph* and *The Daily Telegraph* newspapers and food articles for *Cleo* magazine. She then became Food Editor of *Vogue Entertaining, Vogue Australia* and *Vogue Living*, and now she works from home as Food Director at Large. She has just completed her latest book, with Barry McDonald, *From Market To Table*.

Kirsty Cassidy began her career in catering. She moved into food styling and editing at *Australian Good Taste* and then *Elle Cuisine* magazines. In 1999, she received the Australian Food Writer's Award for best food stylist. She now works as a freelance food and lifestyle stylist.

Elizabeth Chong has been a leading exponent of Chinese cooking in Australia for more than 40 years. In 1961, Elizabeth first established her cooking school, still going strong today. She also conducts gourmet tours of Melbourne's Chinatown. Regularly appearing on Bert Newton's Good Morning Australia and radio, Elizabeth is also the author of eight books, including *Tiny Delights*, which has formed the basis of a TV series of the same name, to be screened on Foxtel.

Pamela Clark's affair with the food industry celebrated its 40th anniversary in 2002. Pamela started in 1962 as a cooking teacher/demonstrator. Since 1969 she has worked for ACP in *The Australian Women's Weekly* Test Kitchen, originally as Chief Home Economist, then Food Editor, and now as Director. Since 1984, Pamela has been responsible for more than 110 cookbooks for *The Weekly's* cookbook series.

Hideo Dekura first visited Australia in 1972 and in 1974, settled in Sydney, where he set up a catering and consulting company, Japanese Functions of Sydney. He gives lectures and is the author of several Japanese cooking videos and cookbooks, including his most recent, *Japanese Flavours, Modern Classics*. He is also a master of literature in Shijyoshinryu.

Stefano de Pieri migrated to Australia in 1974 from Italy. After graduating in politics from Melbourne University, he became an Ethnic Affairs advisor and contributed to the development of multicultural policies in Australia. After marrying, he moved to Mildura, and managed the underground cellar restaurant, now called after him. Stefano appears in the ABC series, A Gondola on the Murray.

Peter Doyle's career spans 30 years — he has been referred to as a 'home-grown legend' and 'inspiration to the industry'. Peter's trademark is contemporary Australian food, which is uncluttered, seasonally-driven and executed with French-influenced precision. In 2003 Peter and wife Beverley moved to est, establishment's fine-dining restaurant, after three years running the multi-award-winning restaurant Celsius.

Betty Dunleavy is a life member of the Food Media Club of Australia of which she was a foundation member. Her extensive career in the food industry included 18 years with AGL and 11 years with ACP as Cookery Editor of *The Australian Women's Weekly*, *The Daily Telegraph*, *The Sunday Telegraph* and various suburban newspapers.

Matthew Evans is a former hatted chef who now reviews restaurants for *The Sydney Morning Herald* Good Living section and *The Sydney Morning Herald Good Food Guide.* He writes the *Good Weekend* magazine's Weekend Fare column (now also appearing in *The West Australian*). He is the author of three books, including the 2001 Vittoria Food Media Club Award-winning *Kitchen Basics*.

Sue Fairlie-Cuninghame is the current joint holder of the 2001 Jacobs Creek Tasting Australia Award for best Food & Wine section within a magazine, which was awarded for work which was published in *InsideOut*. Currently, her media contributions are freelance.

Annette Forrest is a freelance food consultant and stylist. Instrumental in setting up the Sydney Seafood School, Annette promoted Australian seafood for more than 10 years. She has contributed to *Australian Good Taste* and *Elle Cuisine* magazines and has worked as a private caterer in London.

Kay Francis' attitude to food was shaped by travel and growing up in a family of keen gardeners in rural New Zealand. In Australia, she developed a career in catering, magazine food and travel styling and writing. She has written and styled three cookbooks: *A Handful of Herbs*, *Saturdays & Sundays* and *Travelling Food*.

Belinda Franks has the enviable track record of more than 20 years continuous experience in the catering industry. Food and its presentation is a way of life for Belinda. Belinda Franks Catering is well recognised as one of Sydney's leading catering companies, positioned at the top end of the market. For more information see www.belindafranks.com.au.

Margaret Fulton is one of Australia's leading cookery writers and the Patron of the Food Media Club. The author of nine best-selling cookbooks, which have sold more than 3 million copies, Margaret has been a regular contributor to *New Idea* and *Woman's Day* magazines. Her pre-eminence in the food world was given official recognition when she was awarded the Medal of the Order of Australia in the Queen's Birthday Honours of 1993.

Gabriel Gaté trained in some of France's best restaurants. He has been broadcasting on food and cooking on ABC radio for 20 years, writes for newspapers and magazines and has presented cookery on television programs, such as The Good Food Show, Everybody (ABC Television), Body and Soul and What's Cooking (Channel 9), Fun in the Kitchen (Channel 7) and Good Morning Australia (Channel 10).
His 18 books have sold more than one million copies.

Suzanne Gibbs gained a Diploma from the London Cordon Bleu School of Cookery, then became head sweet and pastry chef at the Cordon Bleu restaurant. Suzanne has contributed to *The Sunday Telegraph*, *Woman's Day*, *New Idea* and *Australian Home Beautiful* magazines. Suzanne has written eight cookbooks, most recently *Sweet Things*.

Dorinda Hafner is a very popular regular on Good Morning Australia, every Monday morning with Bert Newton. Her five food anthropology series, and accompanying books, have earned her a rightful place as an international ambassador of fabulous food. The diverse and interesting cultural mix in each half-hour episode leaves us needing much more. For more see information www.dorindahafner.com.

Food stylist **Fiona Hammond** completed a degree in photography before opting to work in front of the camera. For 10 years Fiona has written recipes and styled extensively. She has been the food columnist for *Sunday Life!*, *The Sunday Age/Sunday Sun* magazine. Fiona's aim is to demystify cooking — to inform and inspire the home cook.

Donna Hay has written five internationally best-selling cookbooks and has a bi-monthly magazine and newspaper columns in seven News Limited newspapers in Australia and New Zealand. Her recipes focus on fresh modern flavours, stylish presentation, ease of preparation and readily available ingredients. It's all about turning simple into special. For more information see www.donnahay.com.au.

Ian Hemphill cannot remember when herbs and spices were not a part of his life. Herbie (his nickname since school days) is the author of the award-winning book *Spice Notes — a cook's compendium of herbs and spices* and proprietor, with his wife Liz, of Herbie's Spices in Rozelle. For more information see www.herbies.com.au.

Iain Hewitson has been chef/owner of several well-known restaurants and still operates St Kilda icon, Tolarno. For 12 years he has been seen on TV shows such as Healthy, Wealthy & Wise, A Cook's Journey and Huey's Cooking Adventures. Iain has written five books — *A Cook's Journey, Tales & Recipes from a Travelling Cook, The Huey Diet, Huey's Greatest Hits* and *Huey's Best Ever BBQ Recipes*. For more information see www.hueyscookingclub.com.

Di Holuigue is author of 13 cookbooks, and for 26 years has contributed to many Australian journals. Di was awarded Best Contribution to Food Print Medium at the Food Media Club inaugural Food Writers' awards. Her cooking school, The French Kitchen, has had more than 54,000 students. In 2002, *The Times* (London) Cook called Di 'one of the world's greatest cooking teachers'.

Nigel Hopkins has been writing about the Australian food and wine industry for 15 years. He was food writer and restaurant reviewer for *The Advertiser* newspaper in Adelaide and editor of several editions of *The Advertiser Good Food Guide*. He co-edited *Dine*, a series of restaurant guides to South Australia and assists with the *Australian Gourmet Traveller* restaurant guide.

Peter Howard has worked in the food industry for more than 37 years, as chef, writer, broadcaster and television personality. A past-President of the Food Media Club, Peter was for many years food editor for channel Nine's Today show. Currently he is, Food Editor of Rural Press' *Friday Magazine* and is closely involved with the Royal Agricultural Society of New South Wales. Peter is the author and co-author of several cookbooks, his most recent being *Barbecued!* and *Meat!*

Siu Ling Hui is Malaysian-born Chinese. Although her professional background is in finance, she is passionate about food and has developed a career as a food writer for publications including *Good Weekend*, *Divine Food and Wine* magazine, *The Weekend Fin* and as a reviewer for the *Melbourne Cheap Eats* and *Good Food* guides. She has also organised events for the Melbourne Food and Wine Festival.

Belinda Jeffery is an award-winning TV food presenter, writer, radio personality and cooking teacher who had a successful career for many years in the restaurant industry before joining the food media. Her second cookbook, *Belinda Jeffery's Tried and True Recipes*, was released in November 2002 and she is now working on a third book due out in 2004.

Margaret Johnson is the Food Editor of *The West Australian*, writes for *Scoop Magazine* and *Outback* and is a restaurant critic with *Australian Gourmet Traveller*, *Qantas Magazine*, *Renault Magazine* and the ABC's Radio 720. She has had more than 15 years' industry experience as a restaurant and food consultant. She is also the author of two books.

Simon Johnson began his career as an apprentice chef in New Zealand, achieving the City and Guilds of London accreditation with High Distinction. Later, he began provedoring quality food and now has three retail stores in Sydney, one in Melbourne, a wholesale business, an eponymous brand and is expanding to North America. For more information see www.simonjohnson.com.au.

Undoubtedly one of Australia's national treasures, **Bernard King** burst into the world, spatula in hand, more than 65 years ago. Our cooking style and the way we looked at food changed when King's Kitchen hit the airwaves for almost 20 years (in various guises). Up until his recent death, Bernard was stopped in the street, mobbed at public functions or while he was propped against chic bars and complimented by his adoring fans on the way he changed their eating habits. Bernard wrote four cookbooks.

Max Lake, sometime surgeon, winemaker, writer, researcher and cook, is an Honorary Life Member of the Food Media Club. His most recent book, *Max Lake's Definitive Book on Flavour,* is due in mid 2003. He has been described variously as 'that elder statesman of good taste' (Susan Owens), 'Australia's own philosopher in the kitchen' (John Newton), 'rascal of the senses' (Tim White) 'would make gastronomic poets of us all' (Alan Saunders) and 'the man who started the wine boom' (Cherry Ripe).

John Lethlean is a journalist who became a pie man and cafeteur. The opportunity to review restaurants for the *Melbourne Weekly* led back to full-time writing, then to *The Age* where he had been a cub reporter. He has been its restaurant critic and gossip columnist for five years, and now also reviews restaurants for *Australian Gourmet Traveller*.

Barbara Lowery is a founding member of the Food Media Club, was Chairperson of the Food Writers' Awards in 1997 and has been a judge of these awards. She has broadcast on food on ABC Radio for more than 16 years, has written six cookbooks, contributed to international cookbooks and is a food consultant. She also enjoys playing competitive golf.

Tess Mallos is a freelance food consultant, writer and cookbook author with more than 40 years' experience. While she is a dedicated supporter of Australian-produced foods, evidenced in her *Made in Australia Food Book*, Tess is better known as the author of *The Greek Cookbook*, *The Complete Middle East Cookbook* (in print since 1978), and *The Complete Mediterranean Cookbook*.

Christine Manfield is a chef, author, food writer, manufacturer, presenter, teacher and gastronomic traveller. Since closing Paramount Restaurant, Chris continues to grow as a chef and is regularly invited overseas. She has published four books: *Paramount Cooking*, *Paramount Desserts*, *Spice* and *Stir*. Her collection of spice pastes is available across Australia and internationally. She hosts regular culinary overseas Spice adventures.

Steve Manfredi was born in Italy but established his reputation in Australia at his restaurants, Restaurant Manfredi and bel mondo, in Sydney. He has been an integral part of the development of Australia's culinary identity, and has written two books with John Newton — *Fresh From Italy* and *bel mondo — Beautiful World*. He contributes to *The Sydney Morning Herald* Metropolitan and Good Living sections and *Australian Doctor* magazine.

Luke Mangan started out at Two Faces, Melbourne, and later at Delgany Country House, Portsea, Victoria. After working in the UK at Waterside Inn and Kensington Place, Luke returned to Restaurant CBD, Sydney, before opening Salt restaurant and Fix bar in Darlinghurst followed by Bistro Lulu in Paddington. He is involved in industry events, television, Masterclass weekends, cooking classes, a restaurant consultancy business and Luke Mangan Fine Foods. He is also the author of two books, *BLD*, co-authored by Lisa Hudson, and *Luke Mangan Food*. He is guest Food Editor for *The Sydney Morning Food* and *The Age*.

Anneka Manning is a freelance food editor, writer and consultant. She has spent more than 12 years in the food print media on magazines such as *australian good taste* and *Australian Gourmet Traveller*, and produced books such as *good food* and *more good food* and a range of single-topic, mass-market cookbooks. She believes that the best food is simple food done well.

Kate McGhie was trained as a chef in Switzerland. A supporter of young cooks, she sponsored and trained the first Australian cooks' team to a gold medal win at the World Culinary Olympics. She writes for Melbourne's *Herald Sun* and in 2001 she was Best Writer on Culinary Tourism at the Australian Food Media Awards.

Lyndey Milan is President of the Food Media Club. An energetic, multi-award-winning communicator, author, teacher and presenter, she is Food Director of *The Australian Women's Weekly*, co-host of Fresh on the Nine Network and Councillor of the Royal Agricultural Society. She has written on food, wine and lifestyle for most magazines, newspapers and the internet, appeared on all three commercial television networks and has written four successful cookbooks.

Lynne Mullins is an award-winning Australian food writer and restaurant critic. She has travelled extensively in her quest to master many different culinary techniques and styles. She regularly contributes to *Australian Gourmet Traveller*, the *North Shore Times* and *The Sydney Morning Herald*. She has a fine food review on Radio 2UE, demonstrates recipes on television and gives cooking classes.

As a journalist, **John Newton** publishes in *The Sydney Morning Herald* and *The Age*, among others. His novels are *Whoring* and *The Man Who Painted Women*. His food books include *Wogfood, an Oral History with Recipes; bel mondo — Beautiful World* with Steve Manfredi; *Food the Essential A to Z Guide*; and *The Food Shoppers' Guide to Sydney*, with Helen Greenwood.

Barbara Northwood is a home economist of more than 20 years' experience and Food Editor with *Woman's Day* for the past 12 years. Barbara has a huge following with readers in both Australia and New Zealand. She is well known for her appearances on radio and TV.

Jan Oldham, artist, journalist, home economist and consultant, remembers the forming of the Food Media Club. She has worked for *Vogue, Australian Gourmet Traveller, The Daily Telegraph, The Australian* and *The Sunday Times*, has written cookbooks and conducts cooking classes. Jan's passions include wild and bush foods and the olive. She is working with the University of WA to develop these industries in Western Australia.

Maeve O'Meara is the food presenter on Channel Seven's top rating Better Homes and Gardens. She created and presents The Food Lovers' Guide to Australia with Joanna Savill. She started her own food adventure company, Gourmet Safaris, five years ago and continues to be inspired by the food and culture of people from around the world. For more information see www.foodandwinelovers.com.au.

Anders Ousback commenced professional life as a wine taster, cook and maitre d'. He has owned and operated several Sydney restaurants and cafes, and consulted nationally and internationally. His present interests are The Wharf Restaurant in The Rocks, Yulla in Bondi, The Clock Hotel in Surry Hills, and as CEO of Lynwood Stores. Anders is also pursuing a parallel career as a potter.

Ian Parmenter, former journalist and TV producer/director, is the presenter of ABC TV's 'Consuming Passions'. He has produced 11 recipe collections and a book, *Cooking with Passion*, which won awards in the French Festival Internationale Tele-Gourmande, including the event's Grand Prix in 1996. Ian is Festival Director of Tasting Australia, contributes to *delicious*. magazine and lives and produces wine in the Margaret River region of Western Australia. For more information see www.abc.net.au/passions/.

Elise Pascoe established her cooking school in Melbourne in 1975. After moving to Sydney in 1982 to begin the Fine Food Column for the inaugural Good Living pages of *The Sydney Morning Herald*, her school was based in Sydney's eastern suburbs until 1998. It now operates from Jamberoo Valley, NSW. In 1995, Elise gained Certified Culinary Professional status, the second Australian to do so, from the International Association of Culinary Professionals in North America.

Sydney Pemberton's training began in her mother's kitchen and later continued at the Cordon Bleu School in London. Sydney's enthusiasm for food helped her start her own catering business, Pemberton's Travelling Fare. More than 10 years ago, she started specialising in intimate cooking classes including children's school holiday workshops. Sydney and Kathy Snowball now run snowball&pemberton FOOD WORKSHOP providing market tours and cooking classes for small groups. Sydney has written more than 11 books including the top-selling *How to Clean Practically Anything* as well as *How to Cook Practically Anything*.

Neil Perry is one of Australia's most influential chefs. He has managed several quality restaurants in Sydney and today concentrates on his flagship brand, Rockpool and Rockpool Consulting. He is author of two recipe books, four classical/recipe CDs, creator of a range of food products and a television presenter on The Lifestyle Channel's Food Source. Neil has also recently opened a new Asian-style restaurant in Potts Point called XO. For more information see www.rockpool.com.

Victor Pisapia, chef and passionate exponent of the cuisines of the Americas and Australia, celebrates these through the marriage of traditional cuisines and modern stylings. Former chef of Rattlesnake Grill in Sydney, he now uses his talents as a presenter, educator and chef in his company, Cheeky Food Group. For more information see www.victorsfood.com.

Jan Power is a Brisbane-based cook, writer, broadcaster and operator of a very big and successful Farmers Market. She loves lamb chops best from the culinary cupboard. Available, affordable and easy to cook, anytime for anyone.

Jan Purser is a nutrition consultant, health and lifestyle counsellor, and writer. She is also contributing Health Editor for *australian good taste* and other magazines. For over a decade, Jan has been editing and writing on food, health and nutrition. Jan's latest book is *Indian Home Cooking*, which she co-authored with Ajoy Joshi from Nilgiri's restaurant in Sydney.

Jacques Reymond started in the kitchen of his parents' hotel in Burgundy, France. He studied at the Hotel School in Nice, then worked in England, Provence, Lake Geneva, Brazil, Madrid and Paris. He returned to the family hotel where he received a Michelin star before settling in Australia. Jacques has an award-winning restaurant in Melbourne, is the food and wine consultant to Turtle Island, Fiji, and has filmed a television series for the ABC. For more information see www.jacquesreymond.com.au.

Award-winning journalist, writer and broadcaster **Cherry Ripe** spent her childhood on an English farm where almost everything that was served at the table was grown on the farm. Cherry had culinarily adventurous parents who loved Asian food and eating in Indian and Chinese restaurants on trips to London. She migrated to Australia at high school age and has travelled widely in Asia. Cherry is a food writer with *The Australian*, the author of four books, and has contributed to *The Bulletin, Vogue Entertaining, Australian Gourmet Traveller, The Wall Street Journal*, *The Asian Wall Street Journal* and others.

Sheridan Rogers is an award-winning journalist, author, broadcaster and food stylist. She has worked on several national newspapers, including *The Australian* and *The Australian Financial Review* and written regular food columns for *Mode* magazine, *The Sydney Morning Herald*, *The Age* and *The Sun-Herald*. Sheridan has also written four books, conducted interviews around the world for Alan Saunders' program on ABC Radio National and is currently a regular on Mike Carlton's Drivetime on Sydney's Radio 2UE. For more information see www.sheridanrogers.com.

Nick Ruello grew up in an Italian household in Sydney. His professional career started with 10 years' work as a research biologist with NSW Fisheries, specialising in the prawn industry. The prawn industry remains an important part of his work today as a seafood consultant, and prawns are a favourite food.

Tom Rutherford is a trained chef and principal of the catering and events organisation The Truffle Group whose catering and events, tutoring, food styling, recipe design and professional consultancy are highly sought after throughout Australia, New Zealand and the USA. Tom is often asked what makes the group's events so different. His answer is simple: 'We're different! We are driven by imagination, innovation, and integrity and a desire to give you an event that is truly memorable, one that surpasses all expectations.' For further information log on to www.trufflegroup.com.au.

Brisbane-based **Jeremy Ryland** is a director of The FoodMakers, an integrated television series and internet site targeted at young people, designed to generate a passion for good food and develop simple cooking skills, through education and entertainment while demystifying all aspects of food making.

Christine Salins was Food and Wine Editor of *The Canberra Times* for 9 years until early 2003, when she left to pursue her career as a freelance food, wine and travel writer. A journalism graduate from the University of Southern Queensland, Christine has spent 22 years working on newspapers and is a keen cook, when she is able to escape from the computer.

Barbara Santich is Program Manager for the Graduate Program in Gastronomy at the University of Adelaide. Internationally recognised as a culinary historian and food writer, she is author of six books including *Looking for Flavour* (1996), which won an Australian Food Writers' Award (Best soft-cover food-related book) in 1997.

Alan Saunders is presenter of The Comfort Zone, a show about architecture, design, landscape and food broadcast on ABC Radio National. He is author of *A is for Apple* and his debut novel, *Alanna*, was published in 2002. In 1992, he won the Pascall Prize for criticism.

Joanna Savill is a journalist whose fascination with food began with many years travelling and working overseas. She's since become a dedicated explorer of Australian food, as co-creator (with Maeve O'Meara) of the SBS Eating Guides and the TV series, The Food Lovers' Guide to Australia. She is also a broadcaster, columnist, writer, translator and public speaker. For more information see www.foodandwinelovers.com.au.

Carol Selva Rajah is a chef, consultant, writer, teacher and guide promoting teaching and writing on Asian food and markets in their natural context. She advises companies on product formulations, pastes and sauces and is working to develop a consciousness of beer's natural pairing with Asian food. She is a contributor to the book, *Beer and Food* published in 2002.

Jenny Sheard is a freelance food and travel writer, jazz pianist and singer. During the '80s, Jenny lived and performed in Europe and the United States, gaining invaluable food knowledge from an extended period in Paris and France. Since 1994, Jenny has been a food columnist for *Good Weekend* magazine in *The Sydney Morning Herald*.

Maureen Simpson was Food Editor of *Australian House & Garden* for 30 years and a regular broadcaster on ABC Radio 2BL for more than 10 years. Her first book, *Australian Cuisine*, published more than 15 years ago, was reprinted several times. Her other books include *Cooking at Weekends* and *Comfort Food*.

Geoff Slattery spent most of 20 years (1982–2001) mixing restaurant operations, with sports journalism, publishing, food writing and restaurant reviewing. During that period he was proprietor, or joint-proprietor of five Melbourne restaurants. He wrote recipes for *The Melbourne Herald*, *The Sunday Age, The Age* and the *Melbourne Weekly*, and wrote two cookbooks: *Simple Flavours* and *Good Food No Fuss.*

David Sly is an award-winning food and wine writer from Adelaide, and a recipient of the Professional Certificate in Gastronomy from Le Cordon Bleu and Adelaide University. As a former Food and Wine Editor of *The Advertiser* newspaper, David looked closely at the rise of specialised regional produce in South Australia. He writes for numerous magazines and other publications.

Steven Snow's multi-award-winning seafood restaurant, Fins, is located in Byron Bay, NSW. As well as a chef and restaurateur, Steve is a regular contributor to several magazines and newspapers including *The Sydney Morning Herald*, *The Age* and *Australian Gourmet Traveller*. He conducts cooking classes and Masterclasses and has made guest appearances on both television and radio. For more information see www.fins.com.au.

Kathy Snowball, the former Food Director of *Australian Gourmet Traveller* and ACP Specialist Titles, is a freelance food writer, menu consultant and cooking teacher. Kathy also conducts tours of Sydney growers' markets, incorporating a hands-on cooking class and lunch.

Charmaine Solomon has published 31 cookbooks including the classic *Complete Asian Cookbook* which, 27 years on, still sells worldwide and has been translated into four languages. She has worked on *The Sun-Herald* and *The Sydney Morning Herald* newspapers; *Woman's Day, Belle* and *Family Circle* magazines. She now also produces a range of authentic curry pastes and marinades which are sold in Australia, the UK, USA and New Zealand. For more information see www.charmainesolomon.com.

Jean Storey was one of our first food and lifestyle editors and inaugural Hall of Fame writer for the Food Media Club. She wrote for *The Sydney Morning Herald, The Australian* and *The Sun-Herald* and also edited *Gourmet Magazine* in its early days as well as contributing to various anthologies on Australian food. While her career began in advertising, she has used the family name **Jane Tennant** for her food writing. Travelling extensively, she enjoyed the company of James Beard, Julia Child, Robert Carrier, and Elizabeth David, and other food greats who have visited Australia.

Brigid Treloar is an author, teacher, restaurant reviewer and judge of cookery and recipe competitions. She appears regularly on television and radio and advises many of Australia's top food companies on product and recipe development, food styling and photography and provides recipes, cooking information and tips for company web sites and on-line chat sessions.

Internationally acclaimed chef **Tetsuya Wakuda** came to Australia from Japan in 1982. His first job was as a kitchen hand at Fishwives in Sydney. He then worked at Tony Bilson's Kinsela's, learning classical French technique. In 1983, in partnership with Kinsela's head-waiter, he opened Ultimo's. In 1989 his own restaurant, Tetsuya's, opened in Rozelle, which in 2002, was relocated to the city. There Tetsuya continues to serve his unique cuisine based on the Japanese philosophy of natural seasonal flavours, enhanced by classic French technique.

Loukie Werle is Food Editor of *Australian House & Garden* and *Cosmopolitan*, and a regular contributor to *Australian Table* and *Good Medicine*. Her books include *Trattoria Pasta, The Trattoria Table, Australasian Ingredients, Recipes My Mother Gave Me, Saffron, Garlic and Olives, Balls: The All-Round Cookbook* (with Lyndey Milan) and most recently, *Splendido, The Best of Italian Cooking*. Loukie gives cooking classes in Sydney.

Neale Whitaker is the editor of *Vogue Entertaining + Travel.* He edited *Waitrose Food Illustrated* magazine in the UK and launched the ABC food magazine, *Delicious.*, in Australia. Neale is also a contributor to *Gourmet* magazine in the US.

Glossary

acidulated: rendered slightly sour by the addition of lemon juice.

akudjura: see *bush tomato*.

angelica (glace/candied): a herb, belonging to the parsley family, with pale green, celery-like stalks that have been candied. Used in sweet recipes. Available from health food stores and specialty delicatessens.

amaretto: an Italian liqueur with a distinct flavour of almonds, made from almonds and apricot kernels. Used mainly in desserts. Available from all good liquor stores.

Australian native pepperberry: also known as *mountain pepperberry* or *mountain pepperleaf.* Both the berries and leaves of this Australian native shrub are used. The pepperberries are dark blue to black in colour and have an intensely strong pepper bite that is accompanied by a mineral-like aftertaste that lingers and builds in heat over a period of about 5 minutes after consumption. Available from herb and spice suppliers.

baker's flour: a form of plain white flour that has a higher gluten content than ordinary plain flour, making it more suitable for breads and doughs to rise while proving. To make plain flour behave more like baker's flour, gluten can be purchased and added to the flour — about 2 per cent to 4 per cent of the flour weight. Available from most health food stores or grain specialists.

ballotine (ballottine): meat, fish or poultry that is poached, braised or roasted after being boned out, stuffed, rolled and tied. It is generally served hot but can be served cold.

ban chang koay: peanut crumpets — traditional Malay-Chinese street food.

bean thread noodles: also known as *cellophane noodles*. Made from mung bean, they are stiff when dry but when soaked with water becomes translucent and slippery, hence the name 'cellophane'.

beef tendons: not to be confused with tenderloins. Considered a delicacy by the Chinese, these are the tendons from around the kneecap sometimes with a small chunk of muscle attached. Available from Chinese butchers.

belanga: also known as *chatty* in Tamil. Malay for clay pot or mud pot. The pot is mud coloured and brittle if dropped. It should be soaked in water before using for cooking. When curries, especially fish curries, are cooked in these pots the flavour is amazing. Experienced cooks suggest the belanga, once used to cook fish, should be reserved solely for that purpose.

Benriner: a mandoline or vegetable slicer for finely slicing vegetables.

beurre blanc: literally meaning 'white butter', it is a wine or vinegar reduction into which pieces of cold butter are beaten and shallots added to make a classic smooth sauce. Delicious served with poultry, seafood, vegetables or eggs.

bittersweet chocolate: a lightly sweetened eating or baking chocolate that generally contains about 40 per cent cocoa butter. For superior quality, look for bittersweet chocolate with at least 50 per cent cocoa butter. Chocolate will keep for up to 4 months in a cool, dry place. Available from specialty food stores.

black beans: small black soy beans that have been fermented with salt and spices, they have a strong nutty flavour. Used in steamed, braised and stir-fried Asian dishes. Available in sealed plastic bags or in cans from selected supermarkets and Asian food stores.

brioche: a light yeast bread enriched with butter and eggs.

bush tomato: also known as *akudjura* when ground to a powder, these Australian native berries are pale tan to dark brown in colour with a fruity, caramel-like flavour and slightly tangy acidity. Bush tomato flavours casseroles while the akudjura blends well with coriander seed and wattleseed to flavour meats from chicken and beef to full-flavoured fish, such as salmon and tuna. Available from specialty herb and spice suppliers.

candlenuts: resembling macadamia nuts in shape and size, candlenuts have little flavour. They are rich in oil for which they were originally harvested. It has been said that when candlenuts were first found in northern Queensland, the seeds were pounded, piled onto leaves and lit as candles. The ground seeds are used as a thickening agent in South East Asian dishes. The dried seeds are available from Asian food stores.

cassia bark: also known as *baker's cinnamon, bastard cinnamon* or *Dutch cinnamon*, it is often confused with cinnamon even though the quills are coarser in appearance and flavour. Cassia has a very sweet, pungent aroma and almost bitter taste when used to excess. Available from specialty herb and spice suppliers.

cellophane noodles: see *bean thread noodles*.

chardonnay vinegar: a vinegar made from chardonnay grapes — can be substituted with white wine vinegar. Available from selected delicatessens and specialty food stores.

Charmaine Solomon's Thai red curry paste: available from David Jones' Food Halls and delicatessens.

chatty: see *belanga*.

cherry vinegar: made from steeping cherries in wine vinegar. Available from selected delicatessens and specialty food stores.

chervil: a member of the parsley family, it is quite similar in appearance to parsley although more delicate. Not surprisingly it also has a delicate, parsley-like flavour. Chervil is used traditionally with seafood, in egg dishes and with cream cheese in herb sandwiches. Available from selected fruit and vegetable suppliers.

Chinese rice wine: Also known as *shaoxing* — the Chinese equivalent of Japanese sake (a dry drinking wine) or mirin (a sweet cooking wine). Made from fermented rice. It adds a rich flavour and aroma to all kinds of Chinese dishes and is also used in marinades and sauces. It's colour and quality varies with age. Available from Asian food stores.

choong toy: Chinese preserved turnip. Available from Asian food stores.

chorizo: a coarsely ground pork sausage extensively used in Spanish and Mexican cooking. It is highly seasoned with garlic, ground chilli and other spices. Available from specialty delicatessens, Spanish/Mexican food stores and selected butchers.

compote: a dish of fresh or dried fruit that has been poached in a sugar syrup.

clarified fat: fat or suet that has had the impurities removed. Melt fat in a little water over low heat until all the water has evaporated, leaving only the clear oil, which is strained through a muslin-lined sieve to remove any sediment. When left to cool it will become very hard and white. Lard can be used as a substitute.

couverture chocolate: professional-quality chocolate that contains no less than 32 per cent cocoa butter ensuring that it melts easily and results in a smooth texture and glossy finish. Available from specialty food stores and selected delicatessens.

deep-fried shallots: French shallots that are commonly used in Asia, thinly sliced and deep-fried until they are crisp. Often used as a garnish. Available ready-made from Asian food stores.

demi-glace: A rich brown sauce based on a basic espagnole sauce. Beef stock and Madeira or sherry are added to the sauce, which is then reduced to a thick glaze that will coat a spoon.

dried mango: slices available from selected fruit and vegetable suppliers and health food stores.

enoki mushrooms: a slightly crisp and delicately flavoured mushroom with a creamy white long stem and tiny cap. Will keep in the fridge for up to 5 days if wrapped in paper towel in a plastic bag. If using in a hot dish add at the last minute, as cooking will make them tough. Available from selected supermarkets, most fruit and vegetable suppliers and Asian food stores.

espagnole sauce: sauce made with brown roux or a mirepoix of browned vegetables, herbs, rich meat stock, and sometimes tomato paste.

farce: the French word for forcemeat or stuffing.

fish soy: also known as *Gyosho*, it is a Japanese sauce made from fermented fish and soy sauce. Available from Asian food stores.

flat rice noodles: made of rice, these noodles are flat and about 1.5 cm to 2 cm wide. Commonly used for South East Asian koey teow — noodles tossed with prawns, dark soy and beansprouts. A thinner version, about 0.5 cm wide, is used in Vietnamese pho soups. Available dried from supermarkets and fresh from Asian food stores.

gai laan (kai larn/kailan): Chinese broccoli. A dark green vegetable with broad leaves and thick stems. The peeled stem, sliced diagonally, is used in stir-fries. If the leaves are tender they may be added as well. Available from Asian fruit and vegetable suppliers.

galangal: similar in appearance to ginger, galangal has a fairly smooth skin with a pinkish hue and a creamy white flesh. Its pervading perfume and hot, ginger-peppery pungency is associated with Asian cuisine. It gives Thai food its characteristic flavour and goes well in all Asian curries. Galangal is available from Asian food stores, selected supermarkets and fruit and vegetable suppliers.

garam masala: *garam* means spices and *masala* refers to a mix. Thus garam masala is a very special blend containing fennel seed, caraway seed, cinnamon, cardamom, cloves and black pepper. It is used in Indian cooking in much the same way as Europeans may add mixed herbs to everyday meals. Garam masala adds flavour to curries. Available from supermarkets and herb and spice suppliers.

gari: also known as *beni shoga*, gingerroot that has been pickled in sweet vinegar and coloured bright red. It is used as a garnish for many Japanese dishes, especially sushi, and is also eaten to refresh the palate. Available, in thin slices, shredded or in knobs, from Asian food stores.

gelatine leaves: paper-thin sheets of gelatine. Four sheets of leaf gelatine are equivalent to 2 teaspoons of powdered gelatine. Leaf gelatine needs to be soaked in cold water for about 5 minutes to soften and then squeezed out before dissolving in the liquid from the dish (if hot) or in a little boiling water before adding. It dissolves easily and has the advantage over powdered gelatine that it won't leave behind undissolved lumps. Available from selected supermarkets, delicatessens and specialty food stores.

ghee: clarified butter, used in Indian cooking. Available from the dairy section of supermarkets.

goat's milk: available from selected supermarkets, delicatessens, health food stores and specialty food stores.

gramma: belonging to the gourd family — the same family that gives us pumpkin, cucumber and melon — gramma is often confused with pumpkin. The most common varieties of gramma found in Australia are butternut, butternut large and Japanese (Jap).

green onions: also known as *green shallots* or *scallions*. They have undeveloped bulbs and long, bright-green stems. They will keep for up to a week wrapped in paper towel in a plastic bag. Available anywhere selling fruit and vegetables.

green puy lentils: sometimes known as *French lentils*, they were originally grown in the volcanic soil of Puy in France. Green puy lentils are much smaller than other lentils, dark green in colour and rich in flavour. Available from selected supermarkets and specialty food stores.

green tomatoes: unripe regular tomato varieties, commonly used in Australia in pickles and relishes. Available year round, on request, from fruit and vegetable suppliers. (Not to be confused with the green tomato variety that never ripens and is used in southern American cuisine.)

hazelnut oil: pressed from the whole nut, this oil is full-flavoured and aromatic, tasting of roasted hazelnuts. Store in a cool place for up to 3 months or for longer in the fridge. Available from selected delicatessens or specialty food stores.

holy basil: also known as *tulasi* in India, has mauve-pink flowers, is perennial and is lightly lemon-scented. Available from selected fruit and vegetable suppliers and Asian food stores.

kaffir lime: also known as *makrut* in Thai cooking, it is easily recognisable because of its knobbly skin and unusual double-leaf structure that has the appearance of one leaf joined onto another, end to end. Valued for its aromatic zest and fresh leaves. Most often used in Asian cookery, especially Thai. Available from selected supermarkets, fruit and vegetable suppliers and Asian food stores.

kecap manis: a dark thick soy sauce sweetened with palm sugar, almost treacle-like in texture. It is much sweeter than other thick soy sauces. Used in many Indonesian and Malaysian dishes. Available from selected supermarkets and Asian food stores.

kiln-cooked smoked salmon: usually vacuum packed, the salmon has not only been smoked but also heated in a kiln or oven so that it is lightly cooked. Available in most supermarkets and selected delicatessens.

koshihikari rice: short-grained rice, ideal for sushi because of the way it produces plump moist grains when it is cooked. Available from Japanese food stores.

larb (larp): An aromatic chicken salad popular in northern Thailand. Originally made from uncooked pounded prawns or fish with herbs and lime juice, the lime juice made it possible to eat without cooking. Today the recipe is often adapted for use with other meats.

lard: rendered and clarified pork fat. Available from selected supermarkets, butchers and specialty food stores.

lemon myrtle: one of the most useful Australian native herbs and spices, lemon myrtle has a delicious lemongrass-like flavour and an aroma of lemon verbena. It is available in whole dried leaf or ground form. Use in dishes such as stir-fries and Asian curries as a substitute for lemongrass. Lemon myrtle must be used sparingly, about 1/2 teaspoon of ground lemon myrtle for every 500g of meat and/or vegetables, otherwise the camphor-like eucalyptus taste will dominate. Available from specialty herb and spice suppliers.

lotus leaves: large heart-shaped leaves from the lotus plant. They may be used for wrapping meat and fish parcels and can be eaten fresh or cooked. Dried lotus leaves (dark brown in colour) are also available in packets and may be used in the same way as the fresh leaves after soaking in water. Available from Asian food stores and Asian fruit and vegetable suppliers.

lye water: an alkaline potassium carbonate solution. Used in making Chinese egg noodles and other dough dishes as well as for curing olives. Keeps almost indefinitely. Lye water is very strong so handle it with care. Available from Asian food stores.

makrut: see *kaffir lime*.

mascarpone: a rich double- to triple-cream cow's milk cheese. Delicate and slightly acidic in flavour, it is ivory in colour and thick in texture (can be as thick as soft butter). Used in both sweet and savoury dishes. Available from selected supermarkets and delicatessens.

master stock spices: a combination of spices including fennel, anise, chilli, orange peel, cassia bark, liquorice root and cloves used to flavour a water, soy and sugar combination to be used as a stock in Asian cooking. Available from specialty herb and spice suppliers.

mirepoix: a mixture of onions, carrots and celery finely diced cooked in butter. Occasionally bacon or ham is added. Used in soups, sauces and stews.

mirin: cooking sake made from fermented sticky rice. Available from selected supermarkets, delicatessens and Japanese food stores.

miso paste: made from fermented soya beans, salt and rice or barley. There are about 50 varieties of miso paste available in Australia. They range in colour and taste from the stronger dark paste to the lighter white paste. Available from Asian food stores and selected supermarkets.

mob-cap: a large cap often worn by women in the morning during the 18th and 19th centuries — it had a bag-shaped crown, broad band and frilled edge and came down over the ears covering all the hair.

mouli: a French rotary grater also known as a food mill. It is used for simultaneously puréeing and grating ingredients. Food is forced through a perforated metal disc by a scraper attached to a turning handle.

mousseline: a sauce to which beaten egg whites or whipped cream has been added to give a light and airy consistency.

mushroom parings: traditionally, the parts trimmed off when using whole mushrooms — that is, stalks and peelings. Today, usually the entire mushroom is used, nothing is discarded.

native pepperberries: see *Australian native pepperberries.*

nigiri-zushi: a hand moulded sushi, as opposed to sushi rolled in nori and egg omelette.

Nonya (Nyonya): the combination of the cuisine of Chinese merchant migrants who traveled to Malacca and the cuisine of the indigenous Malays and, to a lesser extent, the cuisine of Indian traders known as Malacca Chetty. The word comes from 'nona', Portuguese for 'grandmother'. Although its origins can be traced to the 14th or 15th century, Nonya cuisine still survives today in parts of Malaysia and Singapore.

oolong tea: made from leaves that are partially fermented resulting in a tea with an aroma, flavour and colour somewhere between black tea and green tea. Available from selected delicatessens, specialty food stores and Asian food stores.

palm sugar: a brown or golden sugar with the texture of crystallised honey, palm sugar is tapped from two sources: the Palmyra palm and the sugar palm, both grown in Thailand, Indonesia, Malaysia and the Philippines. Used grated in Asian desserts and other Asian dishes. Available from selected supermarkets and Asian food stores.

pandanus leaves: also known as *pandan leaves.* Not actually from the huge pandanus tree, but from the fragrant screw pine tree, which has long blade-like leaves growing spirally from the centre of the plant. The leaves are aromatic and when pounded impart a delicate fragrance. The pounded and squeezed leaves can be used to add green colour to foods — one of the reasons why Asian desserts are so often bright green in colour. Pandanus essence (also known as kewra essence) and the leaves are available from Asian food stores.

panna cotta: literally meaning 'cooked cream' in Italian, this luscious, lightly textured eggless custard is set with gelatine and served cold.

pea eggplants: sometimes known as *chilli eggplants*, these tiny green pea-shaped eggplants have a definite bite to them. Used in Asian curries, especially Thai green curries. Available from selected fruit and vegetable suppliers and Asian food stores.

pickled ginger: young ginger is always used in pickling either with vinegar or rice wine because it is more tender and juicy. When sliced it adds a wonderful hot sweet flavour. Available from selected supermarkets, specialty food stores and Asian food stores.

pistachio paste: a concentrated version of the pistachio nut with the consistency of peanut butter, only a little thicker. It should be used sparingly as it has a very strong flavour. Available from specialist food stores and pastry supply shops.

plantain: a variety of banana used for cooking, the plantain is larger than a table banana. Usually cooked when green or underripe. Available from selected fruit and vegetable suppliers.

polenta: coarsely ground yellow cornmeal from northern Italy. Available from most supermarkets.

praline: a confectionery made from toffee and nuts.

pumped: also known as *corned*. Meat such as lamb, beef or pork pickled or cured in seasoned brine.

quandong: often called native peaches, they have a taste a little like a blend of peach and apricot. The thin flesh around the large seed is used in sauces, desserts and garnishes. Also often made into chocolates, jam and chutneys. The fruits, fresh, dried and in products, are available from specialty food stores.

quenelle: small, delicate oval dumpling that is usually poached.

raspberry vinegar: made from steeping raspberries in wine vinegar. Available from selected delicatessens and specialty food stores.

riberries: small, pink and deliciously crisp heart-shaped berries that have a hint of cinnamon and clove flavouring. They are very versatile, being a combination of fruit and spice and can be added to stir-fried dishes, salads, sauces and a whole range of desserts. Riberry jams, relishes, prepared sauces and chocolates, along with whole frozen fruits and delightful sugar-cured products, are available from specialty food stores.

rosewater: a distillation of rose petals that has an intense aroma and flavour reminiscent of its source. Rosewater has been a popular flavouring for centuries in the cooking of the Middle East, India and China. Available from selected supermarkets and delicatessens and specialty Middle Eastern and Indian food stores.

roulade: a flat sponge cake made from a soufflé-like mixture that is rolled up around a filling.

roux: a mixture of flour and fat that, after being slowly cooked over low heat, is used to thicken mixtures such as soups and sauces. The colour and flavour is determined by the length of time the mixture is cooked.

sake: Japanese wine brewed from short-grain rice. Available from Japanese and Asian food stores.

salmon roe: eggs of the salmon. Available from selected seafood suppliers.

sambal oelek: *oelek* is the Indonesian word for pounding and a *sambal* is a chutney or relish. In this case, the sambal is made from pounded chilli and other herbs such as garlic, with perhaps vinegar and salt added to it. It is very hot. Available in most supermarkets.

sansho pepper: also know as *Japanese pepper* — made from dried seedpods of prickly ash. Closely related to Sichuan peppercorns, it is one of the components of 7-spice powder. Used in red miso soup and to combat the fatty flavours of foods such as chicken and grilled eel. Available from Japanese food stores

score: to make shallow cuts, usually in a diamond pattern, over the surface of food.

semolina noodles: noodles made from coarsely ground durum wheat, a highly glutinous wheat. While Neil Perry's noodles are specially made at Rockpool, any good quality fresh durum wheat pasta can be substituted. Available from specialty pasta and food stores.

serrano chillies: red or green, small tapered chillies 4–5cm long with blunt ends. Similar to the small birds-eye chillies used in Thai cooking, except that the serrano chillies are not quite as hot. They are great to use in fresh salsas and for pickling. Available from selected fruit and vegetable suppliers and Asian food stores.

shallots: also known as *eschalots*, *French shallots* or *golden shallots*. They resemble large garlic cloves, grown in clusters and have a tough red/brown skin. They have a strong, nutty and slightly sweet flavour. Available from supermarkets and fruit and vegetable suppliers.

sherry vinegar: a Spanish vinegar available from selected delicatessens and specialty food stores.

shaoxing: see *Chinese rice wine.*

shiitake mushrooms: originating in Japan and Korea, this mushroom has a dark brown cap and is a more delicate-looking version of the common mushroom. The flesh is meaty with a full-bodied flavour. The stalks are tough and are best used to flavour stocks and sauces. Available from Asian food stores, selected super-markets and fruit and vegetable suppliers.

shrimp paste: made from fermented fish, prawns and anchovies. Shrimp paste is principally used in South East Asia but is known by a different name in each country: such as Indonesia — *terasi*, Thailand — *kapi* and Malaysia — *belacan*. Available from Asian food stores.

Sichuan peppercorns (Szechwan pepper/Szechwan pepper): also known as *Chinese pepper, Fagara* or *anise pepper.* Closely related to sansho pepper. Sichuan peppercorns are small, reddish-brown berries that grow on a shrubby tree, rather than on a vine as pepper does. The berries are dried and sold either whole or with the shiny black seed removed. The taste is hot like pepper, lingering and somewhat 'fizzy' on the tongue. It is used in many Asian recipes, especially stocks for duck and pork dishes. Available from herb and spice suppliers.

smoked eel: available from specialist seafood suppliers.

smoked ocean trout with blackening spice: hot smoked ocean trout fillets coated in blackening spice (an Australian cajun seasoning powdered with Australian native pepperberries). Produced by Springs Seafood (www.springssalmon.com.au). Available from David Jones Food Halls and selected supermarkets.

soto ayam: an Indonesian clear spicy chicken soup, also popular in Malaysia and Singapore.

sponge finger biscuits: also known as *savoiardi* or *ladyfinger biscuits*. Made from a sponge batter. They are soft on the inside, crisp outside and readily absorb liquid making them ideal for making desserts such as tiramisu and trifle. Available from supermarkets and delicatessens.

spring onions: these immature onions are also known as bunching onions and have small white, crisp bulbs and long, green stems. Their flavour is more intense than green onions. Trim the tops and roots of spring onions before using. Available from supermarkets and fruit and vegetable suppliers.

star anise: the dried, star-shaped seedpods of this oriental tree are called star anise because of their distinctive and picturesque star shape. Although not from the same family as aniseed, star anise has a similar aniseed taste, it is quite pungent, reminiscent of cloves and liquorice. Available from supermarkets, delicatessens and herb and spice suppliers.

tamarind (fresh): the ripe seeds of the tamarind tree are shaped like large brown peanuts and are found in an elongated brittle pod or shell. There is toffee-coloured flesh surrounding the brown seeds inside the shell. This can be eaten fresh and in many countries it is used to make thirst-quenching drinks. The leaves of the tamarind tree can also be used in soups and coconut sauces. Available in summer and autumn from Asian food stores.

tamarind purée: made from the seeds and surrounding pulp of the tamarind pod. It is sour-sweet and adds a wonderfully nutty sour flavour to any dish. Tamarind pulp concentrate can be purchased in dried blocks packaged in clear packs from Asian food stores. To make a purée soak a piece of the block in water, stir to combine and then strain. Purée in commercial jars is also available in supermarkets.

Thai basil: also known as *hairy basil*, it has slender oval leaves with deep serrations on the edges and a more camphorous aroma than common sweet basil. Used in salads and soups. Available from selected fruit and vegetable suppliers and Asian food stores.

timbale mould: small drum-shaped mould with high sides that are slightly tapered at the base. Used to cook various dishes.

tom yum paste: a Thai paste usually made from the coriander root and stem, galangal and lemon grass blended together. The paste is added to stock to make a hot spicy and aromatic soup. Ready-made paste can be purchased in jars or cans and is becoming more widely available in supermarkets.

truffle oil: oil, usually extra virgin olive oil, infused with truffle. Available from specialty food suppliers.

truffles: prized and expensive fungi that grow from 5–30 cm underground near the roots of trees. Round and irregularly shaped, truffles have thick, rough, wrinkled skin that varies in colour from white to almost black. Fresh truffles are available from Simon Johnson Purveyor of Quality Foods between late October and early February (02) 95522522 or www.simonjohnson.com.au. They are also available canned or in jars (summer truffles) from The Essential Ingredient (02) 9550 5477.

turmeric (fresh): a relative of ginger, it is the rhizome or root that is used in cooking. It has a pungent, bitter flavour and an intense yellow–orange colour. Turmeric is widely used in east Indian cooking and almost always in curries. Available from selected supermarkets, fruit and vegetable suppliers and Asian food stores. Also available dried, as a powder, from most supermarkets.

Vietnamese mint: also known as *poly gonum* or *laksa leaf*. Although it is called 'Vietnamese mint', it is used all over Asia. It has long thin leaves that are aromatic and have a strong bite. Used in salads and laksas. Available from Asian food stores.

verjuice: the fermented juice of unripe grapes. Verjuice has a sour, acidic characteristic and is mostly used to heighten the flavour of dishes, in much the same way as vinegar or lemon juice would be used (although verjuice is more subtle). Available from delicatessens and specialty food stores.

wasabi: a root from Japan, green in colour and very knobbly. When made into a paste it has a bite that goes up your nostrils like hot mustard or horseradish, only stronger. Occasionally available fresh, in Australia wasabi is usually purchased as a tube of green paste or as a powder. Used extensively as an accompaniment to Japanese delicacies such as sushi and sashimi. Available from seafood suppliers and selected supermarkets and delicatessens. Wasabi is now also grown in Tasmania.

wattleseed: also known as *mulga*. There are only a small number of edible wattles, the others being poisonous, therefore the gathering of one's own wattleseed should only be conducted under expert guidance. The wattleseed in culinary use is always roasted and ground, a process that gives it an appetizing coffee-like aroma and taste. Available from specialty herb and spice suppliers.

Index

Alexander, Stephanie	52, 154
Almonds	
pride of Andalucia	98, 99
Anchovies	
flatbread	72, 73
tuna spaghetti with anchovy breadcrumbs	76, 77
Asparagus	
veal scaloppine al limone with	42, 43
Atkins, Mary	24, 154
Australian spices	
Roast chicken with	140, 141
Ballotine of ocean trout	74
Ban chang koay (peanut crumpets)	44
Banana curried triangles	22
Barramundi	
banana leaves, in	128, 129
poached in coconut milk	86
Beans	
chorizo and beans on toast	115
stir-fried crayfish with chilli and black beans	83
white bean purée	80
Beef	
caramelised onions and mustard sauce, with	139
carpetbag steak	37
sugar 'n spice oxtail	142
tendons, Canton style	40
twice-cooked oxtail off the bone	24, 25
Beer, Maggie	119, 154
Beetroot	
risotto with saffron mayonnaise and prawns	122–3
rustic soup	20, 21
Bennett, Sue	50, 154
Bernard's best pumped rack of lamb	138
Berries	
crushed raspberry semifreddo	144, 145
Grandmother's bramble cake	52, 53
mango and berry trifle	100
Truffle cassata	51
Beurre blanc	60
Black beans	
stir-fried crayfish with chilli and	83
Black pepper chicken tea	110
Blackberries	
Grandmother's bramble cake	52, 53
Blood orange and fennel salad with smoked salmon	68, 69
Bloom, Janelle	105, 154
Boon, Jan	22, 154
Bramble cake, Grandmother's	52, 53
Brownies, roast hazelnut	105
Cakes	
Grandmother's bramble cake	52, 53
macadamia coconut syrup	152, 153
orange and almond	98, 99
passionfruit sponge	54, 55
pride of Andalucia	98, 99
ultimate chocolate	102, 103
Calabrese-style meatballs and pasta	34
Calabria, Jo Anne	34, 154
Campbell, Joan	46, 154
Canton style beef tendons	40
Caramelised onion	
beef with mustard sauce and	139
flatbread with anchovy and	72, 73
salmon with tomato and	80, 81
Carpetbag steak	37
Cassata, Truffle	51
Cassidy, Kirsty	66, 154
Champagne jelly	148, 149
Cherries	
liqueur fruit ice-creams with macerated	150
Chicken	
black pepper chicken tea	110–1
chilli mango, with coriander noodles	92
five-spice chicken with lentils	84, 85
I can't believe it's not laksa	127
Kadek's soup	58
larb (Thai chicken salad)	71
Provincial	36
roasted and crusted with Australian spices	140, 141
slow-cooked	79
Thai green curry	89
Chickpeas, curried	
with barramundi in banana leaves	128, 129
Chilli	
chocolate truffles	151
dressing	72
mango chicken with coriander noodles	92
stir-fried crayfish with black beans and	83
Chinese flavoured pork	136, 137
Chocolate	
chilli truffles	151
hot pavlovas with Frangelico sauce and praline	146
iced fruit pudding	104
liqueur fruit ice-creams with macerated cherries	150
mousse	50
Truffle cassata	51
ultimate chocolate cake	102, 103
Chong, Elizabeth	36, 155
Chorizo and beans on toast	115
Clark, Pamela	146, 155
Coconut milk	
barramundi poached in	86
Coconut syrup	152
Coffee butter cream	46

Compote of quail | 28, 29
Coriander
  noodles with chilli mango chicken | 92
  paste | 78
Crab
  easy crab cakes | 23
  mud crab tom yum | 94, 95
Crayfish, stir-fried, with chilli and black beans | 83
Crispy fish skin and nori | 114
Crumpets
  peanut (ban chong koay) | 44
Crushed raspberry semifreddo | 144, 145
Crusted prawns with fennel and Persian feta salad | 88
Curried banana triangles | 22
Curried chickpeas | 128, 129
Curry
  Nonya fish-head | 30–1
  Thai green chicken | 89
Date purée | 130–1
de Pieri, Stefano | 42, 155
Dekura, Hideo | 112, 155
Demi-glace | 130–1
Desserts
  chocolate chilli truffles | 151
  chocolate mousse | 50
  crushed raspberry semifreddo | 144, 145
  goat's milk panna cotta with Champagne jelly | 148, 149
  gramma pie | 48, 49
  Grandmother's bramble cake | 52, 53
  hot pavlovas with Frangelico sauce and praline | 146
  iced chocolate fruit pudding | 104
  japonaise | 46, 47
  liqueur fruit ice-creams with macerated cherries | 150
  macadamia coconut syrup cake | 152, 153
  mango and berry trifle | 100
  passionfruit sponge | 54, 55
  pride of Andalucia | 98, 99
  roast hazelnut brownies | 105
  Truffle cassata | 51
  ultimate chocolate cake | 102, 103
Dorinda's easy crab cakes | 23
Doyle, Peter | 74, 155
Duck
  lychee salad and | 116, 117
  star anise and date purée with | 130–1
Duck egg pasta with kangaroo prosciutto sauce | 119
Dunleavy, Betty | 18, 155
Easy crab cakes, Dorinda's | 23
Eggplant
  tumbet | 26
Eggs
  oyster omelette | 62
  Paul Wilson's eggs with truffles and soft polenta | 60, 61
Evans, Matthew | 127, 155
Fairlie-Cunningham, Sue | 126, 155
Farce | 134
Fennel

crusted prawns with Persian feta salad and | 88
  smoked salmon, fennel and blood orange salad | 68, 69
Feta
  Persian feta salad | 88
Fish
  ballotine of ocean trout | 74
  barramundi in banana leaves with curried chickpeas | 126, 127
  barramundi poached in coconut milk | 86
  crispy fish skin and nori | 114
  garfish nigiri-zushi | 112, 113
  Nonya fish-head curry | 30–1
  salmon with caramelised onion and tomato | 80, 81
  seafood soufflés with Thai flavours | 118
  smoked salmon, fennel and blood orange salad | 68, 69
  smoked trout patties with lime sauce | 82
  tuna spaghetti with anchovy breadcrumbs | 76, 77
  tuna tartare with Melba toast | 120, 121
Five-spice chicken with lentils | 84, 85
Flatbread with caramelised onion and anchovy | 72, 73
Forrest, Annette | 104, 155
Francis, Kay | 106, 156
Frangelico sauce | 146
Franks, Belinda | 88, 156
Fruit see also by name of fruit
  crushed raspberry semifreddo | 144, 145
  date purée | 130–1
  goat's milk panna cotta with champagne jelly | 148, 149
  Grandmother's bramble cake | 52, 53
  iced chocolate fruit pudding | 104
  liqueur fruit ice-creams with macerated cherries | 150
  lychee salad | 116, 117
  mango and berry trifle | 100
  pride of Andalucia | 98, 99
Fulton, Margaret | 98, 156
Garam masala | 86
Garfish nigiri-zushi | 112, 113
Gaté, Gabriel | 100, 156
Gibbs, Suzanne | 96, 156
Goat's milk panna cotta with Champagne jelly | 148, 149
Gramma pie | 48, 49
Grandma Hewitson's lamb shank hotchpotch | 41
Grandmother's bramble cake | 52, 53
Greek-style lamb shanks | 38, 39
Green tomato sauce with spaghetti | 126
Hafner, Dorinda | 23, 156
Hammond, Fiona | 114, 156
Hay, Donna | 144, 156
Hazelnut
  praline | 146
  roasted nut brownies | 105
Hemphill, Ian | 140, 156
Hewitson, Iain | 41, 157
Holuigue, Di | 130, 157
Honey
  spiced pistachio bites | 106, 107
Hopkins, Nigel | 58, 157
Hot pavlovas with Frangelico sauce and praline | 146

Howard, Peter | 37, 157
Hui, Siu Ling | 44, 157
I can't believe it's not laksa | 127
Ice-cream
    liqueur fruit ice creams with macerated cherries | 150
    Truffle cassata | 51
Iced chocolate fruit pudding | 104
Japonaise | 46, 47
Jeffrey, Belinda | 68, 157
Jelly
    goat's milk panna cotta with champagne jelly | 148, 149
Johnson, Margaret | 83, 157
Johnson, Simon | 124, 157
Kadek's soup | 58
Kangaroo prosciutto sauce with duck egg pasta | 119
King, Bernard | 138, 157
Lake, Max | 40, 158
Laksa, I can't believe it's not | 127
Lamb
    Bernard's best pumped rack of lamb | 138
    Grandma Hewitson's lamb shank hotchpotch | 41
    Greek-style lamb shanks | 38, 39
    mustard seed lamb | 97
    roasted rack of lamb with miso | 132, 133
    rosemary-scented lamb cutlets | 90, 91
Larb (Thai chicken salad) | 71
Leek
    seared squid and prawns with red onion and | 70
Lemon mayonnaise | 66-7
Lemongrass
    steamed scallops | 64, 65
Lentils
    five-spice chicken with | 84, 85
Lethlean, John | 60, 158
Lime sauce | 82
Liqueur fruit ice-creams with macerated cherries | 150
Lowery, Barbara | 116, 158
Lychee salad and duck | 116, 117
Macadamia coconut syrup cake | 152, 153
Macerated cherries | 150
Mallos, Tess | 38, 158
Manfield, Christine | 110, 158
Manfredi, Steve | 148, 158
Mangan, Luke | 128, 158
Mangoes
    berry trifle | 100
    chilli chicken with coriander noodles | 92
    goat's milk panna cotta with Champagne jelly | 148, 149
Manning, Anneka | 76, 159
Marinade
    chicken, for | 79
Mayonnaise
    lemon | 67
    orange | 68
    saffron | 122–123
McGhie, Kate | 142, 159
Meat

beef tendons, Canton style | 40
beef with caramelised onions and mustard sauce | 139
Bernard's best pumped rack of lamb | 138
Calabrese-style meatballs and pasta | 34
carpetbag steak | 37
chorizo and beans on toast | 115
Grandma Hewitson's lamb shank hotchpotch | 41
Greek-style lamb shanks | 38, 39
kangaroo prosciutto sauce with duck egg pasta | 119
mustard seed lamb | 97
paprika rabbit | 32, 33
pork with Chinese flavours | 136, 137
roasted rack of lamb with miso | 132, 133
rosemary-scented lamb cutlets | 90, 91
sugar 'n spice oxtail | 142
twice-cooked oxtail off the bone | 24, 25
veal scaloppine al limone with asparagus | 42, 43
Mechouia see Tumbet
Melba toast | 120, 121
Milan, Lyndey | 136, 159
Miso
    roasted rack of lamb with | 132, 133
Mousse, chocolate | 50
Mousseline, green pea | 96
Mud crab tom yum | 94, 95
Mullins, Lynne | 64, 159
Mushrooms, savoury roulade | 18
Mustard sauce | 139
Mustard seed lamb | 97
Newton, John | 26, 159
Nigiri-zushi, garfish | 112, 113
Nonya fish-head curry | 30–1
Noodles, coriander | 92
Nori and crispy fish skin | 114
Northwood, Barbara | 82, 159
Nuts
    ban chang koay (peanut crumpets) | 44
    hazelnut praline | 146
    I can't believe it's not laksa | 127
    macadamia coconut syrup cake | 152, 153
    spiced pistachio honey bites | 106, 107
    roast hazelnut brownies | 105
    toffee | 142
    Truffle cassata | 51
Oldham, Joan | 78, 159
O'Meara, Maeve | 71, 159
Omelette, oyster | 62
Onion
    caramelised, with anchovy flatbread | 72, 73
    caramelised, with beef and mustard sauce | 139
    caramelised, with salmon and tomato | 80, 81
    seared squid and prawns with leek and red onion | 70
Orange mayonnaise | 68
Oranges
    pride of Andalucia | 98, 99
    smoked salmon, fennel and blood orange salad | 68, 69
Ousback, Anders | 79, 159

Oxtail
    sugar 'n spice   142
    twice-cooked, off the bone   24, 25
Oysters
    carpetbag steak   37
    oyster omelette   62
Panna cotta, goat's milk   148, 149
Paprika rabbit   32, 33
Parmenter, Ian   84, 160
Parsley and prawn soup   59
Pascoe, Elise   97, 160
Passionfruit sponge   54, 55
Pasta
    Calabrese-style meatballs and pasta   34
    duck egg pasta with kangaroo prosciutto sauce   119
    spaghetti with green tomato sauce   126
    spaghetti with radicchio sauce   124, 125
    tuna spaghetti with anchovy breadcrumbs   76, 77
Pastry
    gramma pie   48, 49
    Grandmother's bramble cake   52, 53
Paul Wilson's eggs with truffles and soft polenta   60, 61
Pavlovas, with Frangelico sauce and praline   146
Pea mousseline   96
Peanuts
    ban chang koay (peanut crumpets)   44
    toffee   142
Pemberton, Sydney   20, 160
Peperonata see Tumbet
Pepper
    black pepper chicken tea   110–1
Perry, Neil   86, 160
Pie
    gramma   48, 49
    Grandmother's bramble cake   52, 53
Pisapia, Victor   151, 160
Pistachio
    spiced honey bites   106, 107
    Truffle cassata   51
Polenta
    Paul Wilson's eggs with truffles and soft   60, 61
Pork
    Calabrese-style meatballs and pasta   34
    Chinese flavours, with   136, 137
Potatoes
    tumbet   26
Poultry
    black pepper chicken tea   110–11
    chilli mango chicken with coriander noodles   92
    compote of quail   28, 29
    duck and lychee salad   116, 117
    duck with star anise and date purée   130–1
    five-spice chicken with lentils   84, 85
    I can't believe it's not laksa   127
    Kadek's soup   58
    larb (Thai chicken salad)   71
    Provincial chicken   36

    quail in pandanus leaves   134–5
    roast chicken crusted with Australian spices   140, 141
    roast quail with pea mousseline   96
    slow-cooked chicken   79
    Thai green chicken curry   89
Power, Jan   90, 160
Prawns
    beetroot risotto with saffron mayonnaise   122–3
    crusted, with fennel and Persian feta salad   88
    parsley soup, and   59
    seared squid with leek and red onion, and   70
Pride of Andalucia   98, 99
Provincial chicken   36
Pudding
    iced chocolate fruit pudding   105
Pumped rack of lamb, Bernard's   138
Pumpkin
    gramma pie   48, 49
Purser, Jan   150, 160
Quail
    compote   28, 29
    pandanus leaves, in   134–5
    roasted, with pea mousseline   96
Quenelles, cream   74
Rabbit, paprika   32, 33
Radicchio sauce   124, 125
Raspberry semifreddo   144, 145
Ratatouille see Tumbet
Reymond, Jacques   134, 160
Rice
    garfish nigiri-zushi   112, 113
Ripe, Cherry   94, 161
Risotto
    prawn and beetroot with saffron mayonnaise   122–3
Roast chicken crusted with Australian spices   140, 141
Roast hazelnut brownies   105
Roasted quail with pea mousseline   96
Roasted rack of lamb with miso   132, 133
Rogers, Sheridan   152, 161
Rosemary-scented lamb cutlets   90, 91
Roulade, savoury mushroom   18
Ruello, Nick   59, 161
Rutherford, Tom   51, 161
Ryland, Jeremy   115, 161
Saffron mayonnaise   122-3
Salads
    cabbage and bean sprout   142
    crusted prawns with fennel and Persian feta   88
    larb (Thai chicken salad)   71
    lychee   116, 117
    smoked salmon, fennel and blood orange   68, 69
    yabby and watercress   66–7
Salins, Christine   80, 161
Salmon
    caramelised onion and tomato, with   80, 81
    smoked, with fennel and blood orange salad   68, 69
Santich, Barbara   48, 161

Sauces
    Frangelico sauce 146
    green tomato 126
    kangaroo prosciutto 119
    miso 132, 133
    mustard 139
    radicchio 124, 125
Saunders, Alan 28, 161
Savill, Joanna 102, 162
Savoury mushroom roulade 18
Scallops
    steamed lemongrass 64, 65
Seafood
    ballotine of ocean trout 74
    barramundi in banana leaves with curried chickpeas 128, 129
    barramundi poached in coconut milk 86
    crispy fish skin and nori 114
    crusted prawns with fennel and Persian feta salad 88
    easy crab cakes 23
    garfish nigiri-zushi 112, 113
    mud crab tom yum 94, 95
    Nonya fish-head curry 30–31
    oyster omelette 62
    prawn and beetroot risotto with saffron mayonnaise 122–3
    prawn and parsley soup 59
    salmon with caramelised onion and tomato 80, 81
    seared squid and prawns with leek and red onion 70
    smoked salmon, fennel and blood orange salad 68, 69
    smoked trout patties with lime sauce 82
    soufflés with Thai flavours 118
    steamed lemongrass scallops 64, 65
    stir-fried crayfish with chilli and black beans 83
    tuna spaghetti with anchovy breadcrumbs 76, 77
    tuna tartare with Melba toast 120, 121
    yabby and watercress salad 66–7
Seared squid and prawns with leek and red onion 70
Selva Rajah, Carol 30, 162
Semifreddo, crushed raspberry 144, 145
Shanks
    Grandma Hewitson's lamb shank hotchpotch 41
    Greek-style lamb shanks 38, 39
Sheard, Jenny 139, 162
Shortcrust pastry 48
Simpson, Maureen 54, 162
Slattery, Geoff 62, 162
Slow-cooked chicken 79
Sly, David 74, 162
Smoked salmon, fennel and blood orange salad 68, 69
Smoked trout patties with lime sauce 82
Snow, Steven 122–3, 162
Snowball, Kathy 70, 162
Solomon, Charmaine 118, 162
Soufflés, seafood with Thai flavours 118
Soup
    black pepper chicken tea 110–1
    Kadek's 58
    prawn and parsley 59
    rustic beetroot 20, 21

Spaghetti
    green tomato sauce, with 126
    radicchio sauce, with 124, 125
    tuna and anchovy, with 76, 77
Spiced pistachio honey bites 106, 107
Sponges
    passionfruit 54, 55
Squid, seared, and prawns with leek and red onion 70
Star anise, duck with 130–1
Steak, carpetbag 37
Steamed lemongrass scallops 64, 65
Stir-fried crayfish with chilli and black beans 83
Storey, Jean see Tennant, Jane
Strawberries
    truffle cassata 51
Stuffing 79
Sugar 'n spice oxtail 142
Sushi
    garfish nigiri-zushi 112, 113
Syrup, coconut 152
Tennant, Jane 32, 163
Thai food
    chicken salad 71
    green chicken curry 89
    seafood soufflés with Thai flavours 118
Toffee nuts 142
Tomato
    Calabrese-style meatballs and pasta 34
    chorizo and beans on toast 115
    salmon with caramelised onion and tomato 80, 81
    spaghetti with green tomato sauce 126
    tumbet 26
Tom yum, mud crab 94, 95
Treloar, Brigid 92, 163
Trifle
    mango and berry 100
Trout
    ballotine of ocean 74
    smoked patties with lime sauce 82
Truffle cassata 51
Truffles
    chocolate chilli 151
    Paul Wilson's eggs with soft polenta and 60, 61
Tumbet 26
Tuna
    spaghetti with anchovy breadcrumbs 76, 77
    tartare with Melba toast 120, 121
Twice-cooked oxtail off the bone 24, 25
Ultimate chocolate cake 102, 103
Veal
    scaloppine al limone with asparagus 42, 43
Wakuda, Tetsuya 132, 163
Watercress and yabby salad 66–7
Werle, Loukie 120, 163
Whitaker, Neale 89, 163
White bean purée 80
Wilson, Paul 60
Yabby and watercress salad 66–7